Woodworking

A Comprehensive Guide to Learning the Art

(Proven Tips on Making Furniture Using Wood and Wood Pallets)

Edward Akins

Published By **Elena Holly**

Edward Akins

All Rights Reserved

Woodworking: A Comprehensive Guide to Learning the Art (Proven Tips on Making Furniture Using Wood and Wood Pallets)

ISBN 978-1-7750979-0-7

No part of this guidebook shall be reproduced in any form without permission in writing from the publisher except in the case of brief quotations embodied in critical articles or reviews.

Legal & Disclaimer

The information contained in this book is not designed to replace or take the place of any form of medicine or professional medical advice. The information in this book has been provided for educational & entertainment purposes only.

The information contained in this book has been compiled from sources deemed reliable, and it is accurate to the best of the Author's knowledge; however, the Author cannot guarantee its accuracy and validity and cannot be held liable for any errors or omissions. Changes are periodically made to this book. You must consult your doctor or get professional medical advice before using any of the suggested remedies, techniques, or information in this book.

Upon using the information contained in this book, you agree to hold harmless the Author from and against any damages, costs, and expenses, including any legal fees potentially resulting from the application of any of the information provided by this guide. This disclaimer applies to any damages or injury caused by the use and application, whether directly or indirectly, of any advice or information presented, whether for breach of contract, tort, negligence, personal injury, criminal intent, or under any other cause of action.

You agree to accept all risks of using the information presented inside this book. You need to consult a professional medical practitioner in order to ensure you are both able and healthy enough to participate in this program.

Table Of Contents

Chapter 1: The Art Of Joining Wood Is That Requires 1

Chapter 2: Hand Tools 12

Chapter 3: Simple Joinery 23

Chapter 4: The Mortise And Tenon Joint 35

Chapter 5: Display Joints 42

Chapter 6: Dovetail Joinery 45

Chapter 7: Straight-Line Joints 60

Chapter 8: Machined Joints 72

Chapter 9: The Craft Of Joinery Demands 82

Chapter 10: Hand Tool 91

Chapter 11: Simple Joinery 101

Chapter 12: The Mortise And Ten On Join 112

Chapter 13: Display Joint 118

Chapter 14: Straight-Line Joints 134

Chapter 15: Machined Joints 146

Chapter 16: What Is Woodworking? 156

Chapter 18: Tools And Techniques Of Outdoor Wood Project 179

Chapter 1: The Art Of Joining Wood Is That Requires

A certain set of skills of workers, which must develop over the course of. Joinery is a part of woodworking, which is about the process of bringing perfectly crafted pieces of wood together in order to make stunning and complicated wood craft. The creation of joints in wood is done with the help of bindings, fasteners or any other suitable type of adhesive. Unique characteristics of wood joints like design, the flexibility, and their design, and strength are all dependent on the specific materials utilized for joints and also the role of the joint. It has led to different methods of joining that can meet the changing requirements of woodworkers, e.g. what joinery needs to be used for tables are likely to be different than the requirements for the structure of a structure.

Although wood pieces can be joined by using nails or screws, this doesn't provide the long-lasting durability and aesthetic appeal that a beautifully executed work of art ought to possess. Furniture that is joined can be extremely valuable, as well as bringing happiness and fulfillment to owners and woodworkers.

The various types of joints which are well-known meet different needs, and the difficulty and complexity of assembly, no matter how simple or complex, all require some knowledge of how wood joints function.

Wood joinery can be separated into methods that don't make use of any kind of fasteners (the traditional way) as well as the alternative methods. They consist of most often domino joints as well as biscuit joints that go a great way towards improving the strength and appearance of joints by simpleness and elegance.

Traditional wood joinery makes use of the beneficial properties of the wood to prevent the need for external components. The method of joining has undergone small modifications, based on tradition and location in which it is most commonly employed. Joinery found in regions like the Middle East and Asia employ many joints with no glue or nails since these substances can be negatively impacted by environmental factors and do not serve any practical purpose in the system of things. The woods that are found in these areas also have huge amounts of resins which are not in agreement with the usage of glue.

The most obvious sign of great woodworking is joint's strength; you will require precise cuts. It is necessary to use an jig as well as a fence utilization (essential tools for woodworking) when the dissection guiding tool the use of jigs and the tools for cutting required to be guided are saw blades as well as router bits. Jigs ensure the different cuts are completed in a smooth manner, and the smooth and rigid edge on the power saw is sometimes employed to cut the material to be cut is referred to by the name fence.

Each wood is unique and has its unique characteristics. It is even said that they are like humans, but with characteristics which make them unique with respect to their own uniqueness. They are also named upon these characteristics. They are all considered when selecting the wood to use for projects in woodwork.

The classification of woods is three by the composition of the tree they're made from as well as the amount of wood they are. It is essential to know the properties of your wood first in order to identify the proper kind of wood required to achieve the result you want.

Softwood

Hardwood

Engineered wood

Softwoods

Lumber and timber are both softwood varieties derived from conifer tree. Gymnosperms are the name used by biology for conifers. Just as the name suggests they reproduce cones, and have needle-like characteristics. The softwood species that are used for woodworking, crafting as well as cabinetmaking are Cedar and Fir. Redwood, Spruce, and Pine.

Hardwoods

The type of tree that does not produce cones or needles that are produced by softwoods is referred to as hardwood. Deciduous trees are another term for hardwoods. They are scientifically classified as angiosperms. Hardwoods have seeds and leaves.

Cherry, oak, maple mahogany, oak, and walnut are the most common species of hardwoods. The hardwood species may not be the same as softwoods, but various species are renowned because of their appealing and stunning wood grain patterns.

Certain woods can also be referred to as woods, even though they're not deciduous plants, e.g., the palm and bamboo. The plant species are classified as monocotyledons due to the fact that they share the same characteristics as hardwoods and are commonly referred to hardwoods. The palm and bamboo species are rarely considered to be engineered wood.

Engineered Wood

Engineered woods aren't the only kind of wood you can find. They are often frequently manufactured as they are unable to be found in our current surroundings.

The treatment of engineered wood is usually accomplished through heat or chemical process. The purpose of this process is to make the specific type of wood which is able to satisfy specific dimensions as well as unique characteristics that nature isn't able to provide.

Plywood, Oriented Strand Board, Medium Density Fiber Board as well as Composite Board are examples of engineered wood. Wood veneers can be at times thought to be an instance of engineered wood because the manipulation of it has to be performed periodically, and the process can be done using special techniques for cutting or shaping an intricate pattern of grain, or creating a fresh wood that is created by mixing two different types of wood.

Moisture Content and Movement

Wood expands and contracts, and, in the end, it causes movement throughout the piece. It is important to consider the movement before embarking on any undertaking in which the proportion of water in the wood alters, it is moved. The wood of a plant recently felled is green and its cavities contain sap. Sap makes up around 72% of total water content of the wood, and the percentage of this varies with various types of wood. The remaining 28% are composed of wood fibers that in turn, saturate the cell walls of the wood. The size of a sponge increases in the presence of water, the same thing happens for the wood fibers once they are put in a space with a high humidity levels.

As soon as the wood starts drying up as evaporation happens, and the held water or moisture is released. The wood's dimension and structure remain the same until water escapes in the first place, then the contraction kicks into.

Around 4%-11 percent moisture remains in the wood following evaporated. The amount of water content in wood is determined by its environmental conditions. The quantity of water in the natural environment is dependent on the water content to the wood. The two are in direct proportion; which means that a rising of one results in an rise in the other. Wood generally loses around one percent water content per 5percent drop in environmental humidity.

When the moisture in wood increases, so does the wood fiber expands in size. As the water evaporates the wood fiber will shrink. The result is wood expansion and contraction. The increase and decrease of humidity throughout the northern hemisphere both in the winter and in summer. Air conditioning and fireplaces can greatly impact the level of humidity, either inside as well as outdoors. Additionally, humidity varies in a structure from one to the next in the event that the interior temperature differs. Seasonal changes and location can have an impact on the longevity of trees.

Direction of Movement

Wood constantly expands and shrinks. However, the movement of wood across all directions isn't precise. The grain's design allows moving in three distinct directions.

In parallel to the grain of wood There is stability across the entire length. The size reduction of green lumber after drying will be around 0.01 percent of its initial length. This is 3/32 inches, which is the maximum amount performed by an eight-foot longboard. The movement of wood across the grain is in direct relation to the growth of the ring, approximately 8% length loss is eliminated by walking in this direction.

Around 4% of the extension can be observed when looking in radial directions starting at the pith along the radius of the tree. In addition to the reasons mentioned earlier the quarter-sawn lumber is more durability than plain-sawn lumber. The term "tangential dissection" refers to the process that plain sawn lumber goes through. It is a process that causes its motion twice as long as quarter-sawn wood that has the radial dissection. The tangential motion is about 8% however, the radial motion on the opposite side is about 4percent.

Chapter 2: Hand Tools

They don't need electrical power. This is more of the mechanical tools. The tools you can use include clamps, hammers, cutters, as well as many more.

Types of Hand Tools and Usage

Hand tools are required for our everyday activities as examples of these actions that require hand tools include gardening, woodworking as well as many other.

There are a variety of general-purpose hand tools and high-end brands are available for purchase. Hand tools is a necessity for most workshops and homes.

Hand tools that can be used for general purpose are as follows:

Knives

Knives for kitchen aren't the only thing we're talking about in this article. Each toolkit for the home is required to have a premium knife intended for use in craft. The knives are constructed from tough materials that can be used to cut remove letters, boxes, or to cut through less hard substances. For security reasons, be sure that the blade is locking mechanism while it's not in use.

Scissors

Scissors can be found in nearly all homes for various purposes. They've proven effective in almost every situation related to cutting e.g. circumstances such as a school project cooking, in kitchens, DIY projects as well as anything else you require. They can also help for removing seals and packages to be removed.

Screwdrivers

It comes in many dimensions and shapes. It's among the tools that are most commonly used at home. Screwdrivers allow you to fasten and bolt screws to surfaces, fix hinges, and install lights and lamp holders when making cabinets. The screwdriver comes with diverse blades of diverse widths designed specifically for purposes. It is made of carbon steel and is then subjected the heat in order to improve its toughness. The handle is constructed using a specific plastic material that ensures a solid grasp.

Hammers

The device is designed to exert massive force over an area of a tiny size. It is made up of a wood stick, which is connected to a steel block. It is employed to secure nails, break down objects into smaller pieces or forging them into metal. The hand tool should not weigh a lot, which means the effect can be fully utilized when nail nails are secured to the wall. The hammer needs to be adequate in size to the beholder to allow for effortless moving and use in a comfortable manner without discomfort.

Wrench

For holding securely and turning things, wrenches are used. They are essential in securing woodwork, or for repairing bicycles, where they can be used to loosen or tighten nuts or bolts for plumbing, where they're employed to turn pipes. A variety of wrenches is made by hand tool makers that meet the various demands of woodworkers.

Pliers

They're hand-tools of the past that are found in many homes, in some cases, but not all. They're used for holding objects in place, taking off screws and bolts as well as bending certain material. Most often, the material they can bend, straighten, or even cuts is wire. Pliers equipped with needle-nose tips and cutting capabilities are the finest tools one can have. These are hand tools that can be used for both purposes because they are able to be utilized for home use and during workshops.

Clamps

It's a tool used that is used to hold objects together with a firm grip to stop the movement of objects or to prevent separation by the use of an inward motion. The hand-tool may be ad hoc, as they're only employed for holding wood pieces still while you work on them. They may also be fixed, but. Most often, they are utilized to perform repairs or to assemble woodworks or projects for DIY.

Chisel

Chisels are among the most frequently used tools throughout the history of woodworking. Chisels are made of steel and have a blade that is connected to a picket or a plastic handle. Chisels used together with hammers and mallets are typically used to cut, separate and cut wood. Chisels are typically employed to create joint joints in woodwork as well as making the wood.

Chisels typically are used to smooth the wood's surface, making cutting cuts that paring. Paring is a method used to remove the wood's levels piece by piece by slicing the wood. used. There are many ways to get out the wood by slicing the wood's surface with only hand pressure or by taking smaller pieces away hitting them with a deliberate mallet or chiselhammer. The most common reason for this is how far the chisel is able to go deep into the wood. This can be altered according to the angle that the chisel is able to make with the surface of the wood; the more steep the angle, the more it is that the blade pierces the wood's fibers.

It is important to have trust on the pressure applied by hand for cutting wood. Use each hand to hold the chisel into the wood. The dominant hand is placed on the handle, as well as alternately wrapped around or pressing on the blade move the blade with a cutting movement into the wood.

Another reason to use chisels is splitting cutting. This could be where you need to put the edges to cut along the grain of the wood and then hit the handle using mallets. The chisel is pushed into the fibers that are on the grain, separating the wood in pieces rather than shavings. This could be a fantastic method of quickly eliminating a large amount of substances, but it is limited to the directions of your grain if it's not aligned or in your favor.

Cut chopping is a method of cutting directly through the grain usually perpendicular to it however, not in a continuous manner. This is a technique employed to cut mortises as well as various recesses. With a hammer, in the event that the chisel isn't able to penetrate the wood, you should think about putting the chisel with a different angle. This technique is best used when taking off the wood pieces in a gradual manner.

Types of Chisels

There are numerous common kinds of Chisels. The most popular type is the one with a bevel edge. It is usually the best to use in carpentry tooling However, if you've one of these options, it will help accomplish the job, however they may not be as adaptable:

More firmer cut

Butt chisel

Mortise chisel

Power Tools

They are machines or devices that are powered by humans with the help of other sources of energy. This includes pneumatics, electric motors that are powered by gas Internal combustion engines and much more.

If you are considering the use of power tools usage should be limited to certain areas, and care should be taken when the tool is employed in the house. However, the equipment you purchase must have specific features as well as environments where it can use safely along with a myriad of other features specific to the device.

Different Types of Power Tools and Their Uses

Air Compressor

The tool is based on an underlying principle. This method involves turning energy, stored in a compressed air compressor, into the energy that is needed to perform. If you use the compressor's air supply the compressor starts by storing an air reservoir until it is at the maximum capacity. This capacity could differ depending upon the type of compressor that you buy since there are various versions.

This type of power tool is ideal to paint sprays, house and work-shop cleaning, filling car tires, as well as gas cylinders for cooking. This tool can also be utilized to charge a variety of pneumatic instruments, like nail guns, specially-designed kinds of hammers and many more.

Trimmer

If you're looking to create a garden that looks beautiful and attractive All you'll need to do to do it is a quality trimming tool. Trimmers make use of flexible monofilament lines, rather than a conventional blade. It can be used to cut grass, cut other items that can be cut close to plants as well as manage irregular landscapes. The trimmer is powered by gasoline however, at present, electric motor trimmers are on the marketplace. It is typically used to trim grass and giving it appearance and a pleasing structure in cutting a sloping area of ground. Additionally, it is possible to utilize it for different methods of cutting in the field.

Table Saw

For instance, if you want to cut cuts or cutting anything; Table saws are the ideal type of power tool to use. Table saws are equipped with the sawing device underneath an table that has blades which enable you to quickly move across the table. The power source of the table saw comes by electric motors. It is able to be moved easily onto the site where it will be cutting since it is equipped with a ability to move. It is useful when cutting deeper that cannot be done using a saw or any other powered saws.

Drill

Perhaps you've come be aware that this is one of the most useful tools within our homes. Today, there are a variety of different kinds of drills you could utilize to accomplish many tasks. Drills can be used to accomplish various tasks including to put up paintings to the walls, create furniture wooden furniture, metalwork, construction, and much more.

Chapter 3: Simple Joinery

Simple joinery is one of the most well-known method of joining wood together. In this article it is possible to discuss what follows:

Wood Grain and Strength

The term grain is a reference to the direction of fibers made up of wood; it differs from the picture. The distinctive design which is often a result of different grain types. Any grain variety, excluding straight grain can be either a blessing or curse. In the end, lumber that isn't straight grain may be used to create an beautiful designs; however, the errant grain can be beneficial. When it comes to structural projects, for instance the construction of homes, timber (mostly softwood) that has straight grain loss some of its strength. The hardwood lumber with no straight grain require additional attention when machining in order to avoid the possibility of tear-out or other unintentional reaction.

The direction of grain of wood important when working with wood?

Wood is regarded as an organic substance, which is much stronger when the grain runs in a continuous. It could be a naturally occurring as well as a chemical. It is made up of multiple strands of polyose fibers that are held together with an adhesive made of polymer. Consider lining thousands of straws all put together into a linear manner. If one straw isn't strong and weak, the other straws can compensate with strength and will strengthen the whole collection. If you break wood across your grainline, it's breaking up polymer bonds (easy) and when you split across the grain, it's breaking polyose fibers, which have a much greater durability.

In order to take advantage of the maximum benefit of wood's strength

Focus your attention in the direction that grain is moving.

Continue to orientate the grain so that the fibers to take on the weight.

If you can Cut the wood in such a way that the grain runs in a continuous fashion across the entire long length.

Types of Simple Joinery Dados

Dado is an efficient and effective method of connecting two pieces of stock. Once you've learned how cut a dado you'll see that these joints can be extremely useful for building shelves or cabinets.

A dado could be defined as an opening cut in an object of wood to ensure the other piece of wood will fit in the groove with a firm grip. In the case of building shelves made of with a thickness of 3/4' it is possible to cut an inch large groove to the appropriate dimensions of the shelf. Then utilize adhesive to connect the shelf with the groove created.

Techniques for Cutting Dados

Methods used for creating the dado differ. One of the most popular methods is to place a dado head cutter onto the table-mounted saw. This is comprised of 8 to 10" diameter 1/8"-kerf saw blades that have about 1/16" to 1/8" chips in between. By adding or taking out chips, you'll have almost the entire breadth of a groove that is between 1/4 3/8" and 3/4 inches.

Dadoes that are much larger can be cut by making several passes on the saw. The type of dado cutter referred to as a stacked dado head cutter is only employed on a table saw or the radial arm of some saws. Avoid using the type of dado that is stacked on a circular saw because this could be very dangerous.

A different option to the dado set that stacks is the set of wobble dados. It is essentially the saw blade that's mounted on a spindle that can be moved. Adjusting the angle of the blade's position on the spindle alters the width of the dado. It is more affordable contrasted with the stack type.

The results of this set aren't reliable and are based on the things I've experienced, They are not always suitable.

It's a challenge to keep myself from buying the wobble dado, and to save my money to buy the type that is stacked. Additionally, I'm not comfortable using a wobble set.

Cutting Dadoes with a Router

The most well-known method for cutting dadoes is to make utilization of a properly aligned dissecting piece using an router. When you use a router for dissection of a Dado be aware that you could need to slow down the speed of the bit just a bit and then try to fix the depth for several passes to prevent them from scorching the material or burning the bit.

Use a properly aligned edge to monitor the guide. This ensures that you have a straight piece. It is important to note that the 1/4" router bit type will dissect a dado a little larger or more significant than a 3/4" sheet of plywood. While 23/32 bit types are easily available and available, using a the 1/2" bit along with a couple of passes gives the expected result.

Edge joint

The edge-to-edge joint is an extremely common type of joint. The majority of the time, it is utilized to connect tables with different sizes with the same thickness when biscuits joints are used across board's smooth edges.

In order to join tables made from various boards, place the boards in a row by directing each board's grain toward the board's initial direction. This helps to maintain the stability of your tabletop in either contraction or expansion.

The joints will immediately be in the proper position. Use the pencil to draw the marks every 4 to 6". The marks would be the centers of the biscuit slots.

Next step is to complete the separation of the board and then establish the biscuit joiner to the acknowledged dimension of the biscuit joint. If this is an instance of edge cases it is likely that a huge number of 20 in size will be utilized.

Installing the guide fence onto the top of the stock, be sure to align the cutting guide in line with the marks you made using a pencil before. Securely secure the fence place, start to see as you go, and then when you are at the maximal speed, slowly push the blade into the wood until the point that it's impossible. After that, remove the blade entirely and do the same following the pencil marks.

After each space has been cut and a bit of glue should be applied to each edge prior to putting the biscuits in. Place a tiny amount of glue to the remaining areas directly along the edges before gluing the two boards.

Perhaps you decide to hurry adhere each and every edge of the table top and later join the whole piece. It is important to make sure that the clamps are tightly pressed to ensure that each space will be fully sealed. However, you must be careful not to squeeze too hard to keep glue from falling out. If the glue spills, be sure to clean it up carefully to prevent an unsightly finish.

Coopered Joints

Staved containers come in various sizes and styles including firkin and hogsheads with barrels between. Coopers are the biggest plan of any. The 6/5 foot coopers ' jotter looks upwards with an upper end of the wood lying on the floor, while the second one of the jotter, opposite, is raised on a set of legs. The Cooper procedure is performed with the help of an eye, securing each of the staves at precise bevels. Once repetition on the opposite stave occurs this makes an excellent cask.

Every stave is asymmetrical in its angles. And the angle of 90 degrees. When a stave is moved to an jointer, the Cooper returns it with drawing knives to match the shape of the case. It's just the same as a segment of a circle and each edge's exact angle is straight-on to the circle's tangent. It maintains a straight degree of 90°. However wide the stave, observing angles that are right to the tip of the circle creates an unique stave. It is recommended to repeat this process many times until you are sure of the perfect result.

The cover work that is assigned to the joiner includes items like porch columns as well as circular chests with tips. The procedure for joiners is similar to that employed by coopers. Start with normal stock and eggs. Once the eggs are bent, and adhesives must be placed and turned to round out the outside area. Every edge's bevel is equal to the angle between the faces of the stock.

The full-size drawing must be done on sheet and then derive angles from it, however should you want to work more in a scientific manner, you can divide the circle using angles 360 and as many staves that you want to work with.

If you had eight staves, you'd have 45 degrees for each one, which means that each stave will require a straight line that would turn its directions toward the circle. It is important to consider the angle inside; However, 180 degrees is now 135 degrees, after the 45 degrees may be subtracted. Half of 135 equals 67.5 degrees. The eight staves that are of the same length along edges that have below beveling that is 67.5 degrees can give birth to a circle or likely an octagon that could be easily transformed into the shape of a circle.

When the angles be calculated after which they have to be positioned in a precise and continuous manner on every edge. However the square provides a 90-degree fixed angle however the bevel that slides can be locked and set at whatever angle that you wish to. If you have a five-sided item that you want to lock the angle at 54 degrees. edges should be tested when the planes are stitched. The length of every starve must be equal, and it's not possible to carry your plan in case you've made the angles excessively extreme. Often, you plan out excess, mostly because where the stop should be wasn't obvious.

Rabbet

The rabbet is a different one that's cut around the edges of the board, instead of its central. It is often used to join edges so that they fit to each other securely.

Groove

It is possible that you have used interlocking siding or wainscoting far back. If so, you'll know how to distinguish a tongue and groove wood joint. This type of wood joint used for in order to keep boards in place on the edges rather than across their edges. One end is bent by protruding parts known as the tongue. The second part is made by carving an opening called the groove. The two join together securely.

The joint must be secured securely by adhesives. Typically tongues and groves are cut in an acute angle, so that the woodwork must be joined with an angle, and moved down so that the joint is secured. It's easier to complete this procedure with the right router bits. Hand planners can be useful for carrying out these procedures. When working with wood, a groove may be a slot, or trench that is dissected into a piece of wood that is aligned to the grain. One of the main differences between a dado and groove is the fact that a dado flows through the grain whereas an angled groove runs along it. Grooves can be used to serve a variety of functions in cabinetmaking as well as other woodworking related fields.

Chapter 4: The Mortise And Tenon Joint

These joints have been utilized to make woodwork for centuries by skilled craftsmen from across the globe particularly those joints joined are at an angle of approximately 90 degrees. These joints are durable and easy to use in their basic form, and are available in various types, each serving various purposes. The most basic and popular form of mortise and Tenon is comprised of the tenon tongue as well as a mortise opening. The tenon can be crafted, and usually the extension of rails, and is then made into the shape that you desire on the opposite wood item. It should have the perfect shape for the mortise holes as well as to make sure that it won't shift or fall to pieces, shoulders are inserted on top. Alongside the shoulders, various forms of materials or devices could be employed to fix the joint like a wedge, pins or glue. In addition to carpentry and woodworks, this type of joint can also be used by stonemasons and blacksmiths.

Below are various mortise varieties which you can use to complete your projects.

Half-dovetail mortise that has been wedged with an rear face that has an enormous surface area when compared to the opening on the front. The opening lets the tenon in and, however, when the wedge is at work this tenon cannot be removed after it has been the wedge is in place.

Stub mortise. This type of mortise is not as any depth when compared with different mortises. It is not able to traverse the wood piece it only runs an undefined distance.

Through mortise. In this case the mortise is completely into the wood part.

The mortise can be seen open from the highest section of the timber and usually has three sides.

Blind mortise. Here the tenon has been fully in the mortise, and can't be seen. The mortise is often being used to construct of tables and chairs.

Tenons are extensions to pieces of wood which are put into holes known as mortises. The length of the tenon will be significantly greater than its size. Tenons can be of various kinds;

Through Tenon, it passes through the hole, and it can be seen clearly from the opposite side.

The Biscuit Tenon is as a biscuit.

Tenon loose; this kind of tenon can be used independently of the joint that it is working on since it's not fixed directly to the main components of the wood pieces that are which are linked.

Tusk tenon. Here, wedge-like device is utilized to hold the joint securely.

Pegged tenon is sometimes referred to as the pinned Tenon. The pin is put into the mortise or the tenon.

The tenon's dimensions are influenced by how big or tiny the wood. It also is wider compared to the tenon. This hinders the tenon from showing.

It's common that the dimension of the tenon as well as mortise in proportion to the width of the timber. The best practice for woodcrafting is to be about 30 percent of the width of the rail done with.

MORTISE AND TENON EXERCISE

A mortise and tenon could be created using the help of a router table. Follow the steps below:

1. The pieces of wood that will be joined will be cut to the size you want; make sure that the end of the board to be cut in the tenon is exactly at an angle of right angles. With the Try Square place the wood to serve as the tenon onto one side of the timber that will be the mortise, and then mark the length of it.

2. The mark should be three quarters of an inches off from the bottom and top of the line you traced on the mortiseboard in the step 2 earlier. It will be the starting and ending place in the mortise.

3. The thickness should be measured at one-third of the mortise boards both sides, and mark it accordingly. This gives you the length of the mortise.

4. Take the router's narrowest straight tooth. Cut into the mortise. Make note of

the starting and stop points that were initially noted at the top of the process. Begin by cutting slowly, beginning by using the smallest tooth on the router and raising it until a 1-inch mortise is made.

5. A third of the thickness is used to mark the Tenon. Then, the wood is pushed over the router's quarter-inch tooth to one side, gradually until a depth of one inch is reached. The wood is flipped then repeated on the opposite side.

6. Check for suitability and then adjust to suit your needs. Adjust.

NOTE:

This measurement is applicable to an extremely thin block of wood. The measurement can be altered according to the wood's thickness being used and also the amount of weight that the joint is designed to support.

A method for mortise or tenon construction allows you to make the mortise before building the tenon. A tenon is easily adjusted to accommodate a mortise however, a mortise cannot adjust to fit the 10on.

The Bridle Joint

There are many similarities between the mortise as well as joint tenon and the Bridle joint. On one side, the tenon is split in two, while at the other side, the mortise has been designed so to allow the tenon to fit easily. This joint will discover a few types of adhesive that help providing support, and preventing the racking and other unintentional acts. If you want to provide additional help, try using nail or pins to ensure that the integrity of your joint is preserved.

Chapter 5: Display Joints

The Butterfly Joint

The joint is ideal to hold boards in place, or it is a great option for boards that are already joined, however are having certain kinds of issues using the jointing method. In addition to securing boards may also see butterflies joints that are used as decorative, structural or various other purposes. Most often, the butterfly joint comprises of wood that's not exactly similar to the original wooden piece that has been crafted. A hole is created in the wood piece and then the butterfly joint gets installed into it, anchoring the two boards. They also help keep cracks at bay as well as increase the stability of the boards. The examples of these type of joint are in dahshur vessels, Dutch tabletops in the 18th century, and so on.

Bevel top Dovetails

The joint can be used in order to join various pieces by softening edges, giving a more attractive appearance as well as safety benefits. For woodworkers, this type of joinery can also be employed to make relatively tiny dimensions that cannot be easily changed by weather conditions.

Puzzle Scarf Joint

Perfectly-fitting interlocking designs are created in two separate pieces that are joined, with the proper adhesives used, and finally secure. The form that joins and gives the name the type of joint closely mimics how you put your fingers together to secure your fingers together and lock. Interlocking joints provide an ample surface for the use of adhesive. This makes it a durable and sturdy joint. Be sure not to think of a box joint as one that is a puzzle. The latter is often being used to construct doors as well as flooring boards.

Chapter 6: Dovetail Joinery

True woodworkers are recognized through dovetail jointery. Dovetail joints that resemble fingers have a reputation for strength and allow for a solid robust, sturdy and long-lasting fitting. They don't require an external fastener. This makes them ideal for furniture as well as other woodwork.

Two different parts of a dovetail joint. the two components are the pins and tails. The tails are like a dove's tail, while on the flip side and on the opposite edge of the board is the features that are attempting to get between the tail in order to create an unbreakable joint. quickly separated. Continue to add adhesives and join to the joints firmly so that it becomes impossible to split.

Evidence suggests that dovetail joints have been used for quite a while and are found in antique stores. If you go to an antique store where you can easily remove drawers or different furniture to discover that the majority of furniture was made using dovetail joints.

Dovetail joints have several advantages, one of being that it is the most durable of joints. It is a big adhesive surface and is secure, resists to separation, and looks attractive and does not require glue to keep it in place securely.

Dovetail joints are that they could be difficult to trace to cut and mark, and when the construction is poor the joints can be unable to provide the benefits making use of them as mentioned earlier.

It is dependent on the project. There are various dovetail designs that you can choose for your project. Selecting the correct design for your particular project is not just a way to improve the skills of your team, but will also enhance the capabilities of your team.

These are the various kinds of joints that dovetail:

Dovetails that are lapped

There are a variety of dovetail joint. Most commonly, it is a lapped or sloping dovetail. It conceals the joint on the one side, yet make it visible on the opposite side. The most common usage is when it comes to the design of drawers. In this case, the joint's force is needed to connect the sides to the side of the drawer, but they don't want the drawer's front view to be revealed as the drawer closes.

It's an extremely difficult joint to break down. It's a lot like the dovetail through, with only the lap joint can make the waste that accumulates a little more challenging to dispose of entirely off the pin. In order to cut a laced dovetail it is necessary to use the following tools: be required:

Marking gauge

Sliding bevel

Template for marking

Dovetail saw

Coping saw

Writer or scriber

Bevel-edge Chisels

Sliding dovetail

For woodworkers everywhere, the sliding joint is sturdy and dynamic when it comes to application for everything from case-building and rail joining. Most likely, you've seen what the appearance of a sliding dovetail. It's a mix of a dado as well as a dovetail. There is a scratch on one side, and one side having a tongue. side. As both wall dents are also known as groove walls and since the tongue's sides are angled like dovetails, the joint's assembly has to be accomplished through sliding the tongue into the groove's side from an the other end.

The canted walls are prone to give the slide joint an edge over the dado. The joint is able to resist mechanically, which is why the board at the tail is unable to move away from it's groove. Without adhesives, the two parts stay connected. To break them apart it is necessary to crush the wood. crushed.

The joint's design helps in assembly tasks. There is no chance of destroying parts when working using clamps. Two hands are typically sufficient for assembly even in the event of multi-parts, similar to the drawer chest. Panels with a slight bow may be pulled into lines with no flimsy clamping arrangements.

Another benefit of the dovetail that slides is the fact that it allows the pieces to move, without being able to be separated if they are not glued. A good example of this is the breadboard's end. Applying thin wooden strips at the ends of a panel that has been glued to conceal its grain at the end permits it to stay completely flat. Ungluing the joints allows the expansion of table top. Dovetails that slide make extension table slides, as well as join shelves on the opposite sides of a bookcase.

Dovetails that are blind

Dovetails that are blind, and there are:

Dovetails with half-blinds

Woodworkers often utilize a "half-blind dovetail' whenever they need complete obscurity of the finish grain in front part of joinery. Tails are securely seated in mortises at the top of the board which is at the front of the timber, concealing their edges.

Half-blind dovetails are the most commonly utilized for drawer fronts and sides. This differs from the common practice of fitting fake fronts on drawers constructed with dovetails.

In the case of coupling two pieces of wood, the most commonly used joint used is a through dovetail. Dovetails that are through are strong and captivating, however there are a few instances that dovetail joints aren't the ideal.

In the case of connecting of the side of a drawer towards the front of the drawer, you shouldn't make the use of a straight dovetail joinery, since their tail ends are likely to be visible through the front of the drawer.

For this situation, the best dovetail joint for use is the dovetail with a half-blind.

The half-blind or dovetail is extremely precise. As it's referred to, one part of this joint is able to be observed, while the opposite remains hidden. The joint is as rigid similar to the dovetail through, however it is used for situations such as the drawer front example that we have discussed previously.

Making half Blind Dovetails Local methods to create half-blind Dovetails doesn't offer much distinction in the method for creating dovetails through However, there are some things to be aware of:

The part that's not being cut can be referred to as the lap. The lap that is placed in the pin board should be no smaller than 1/8" but should, regardless, possess more that 1/3 board's thickness. This will help ensure the dovetail's durability.

Mitred Blind Dovetail

This joint may also be called the mitered dovetail with full blind or the dovetail with a full blind as it is utilized in intricate woodwork as well as cabinet design. The exterior portion of this joint is constructed to ensure that it cannot be visible when you look closely at the joint. The joint is made in a way that only its interior section that meets with 45 degrees can be observed with a close-up.

How to cut dovetails

1. The woodblocks should be cut to be joined at the same length and make sure both edges are round. Make sure that they are square with your Test square.

2. You can sand the surface you'd like to mark inside, and then mark them according to the markings. Use a measuring gauge could be useful.

3. Adjust the marking gauge at the same thickness as the blocks and draw a line along the edges you wish to join, drawing the front and back and two edges. It is helpful when the gauge is set slightly higher than the size of the block, but not more than 1/32. This creates an extension of the pins as well as ends above the block. Once it is finished and glue-up the extension allows

for a few sanding strokes for a perfectly-shaped corner.

4. Choose the block of wood from which the pins are made from. In general, it is more straightforward to cut the pins before cutting them out. When deciding on the woodblock that is holding the pin, be aware that dovetail corners are able to be separated with only one edge. For security, make sure your cut follows the pull direction. One good illustration is one drawer. The pins must be placed in the front block, and they should be on the sides. This way, you're certain that the joint will remain in place regardless of the pulling.

5. Next, decide the dimensions of the pins you want to utilize. Pins typically are two-thirds the length of tails. It is possible to alter this. If you are determining tails and pins size, be aware the fact that long tails weaken joints. The same is true for excessively narrow tails.

6. Then, place the block of wood in a vice, and then cut it by using the backsaw. This is done following the lines made by the step 3 earlier.

7. Utilize the chisel tool to tidy off the edges of the tail to make them straight and clear. Avoid slicing in the vise, instead clamp it onto an even area instead.

8. Place the pins on the block of wood on which the tails will be cut. Take note of the drawn gauging line, mark the pins. The block must not shift from the moment.

9. The lines were cut and then smooth them with a chisel like described in step 7.

10. Connect the pin to the tail by tapping gently to check the joint's fit. If the pin is not tight enough the joint will not stay in place. If it's too tight the joint could result in splits.

11. Once the fit has been evaluated and verified to be in good order Then glue the seams and join.

12. The edges should be sanded around the joint to create an even finish.

Notice: Two blocks of differing thickness are able to be joined. However, in order to do this there are two distinct setting for marking gauge are required that are for the thickness of the woodblock that you want to join.

Dovetail bandsaw construction

Bandsaws are a useful instrument for woodworking that is that is used to cut shapes, cutting short pieces crosscut as well as the construction of legs cabriole, etc. But, it is preferred in cutting of shapes which have irregular shapes, cutting wood into smaller and more easily manageable pieces, allowing seamless cuts, and so on.

The typical bandsaw is composed of wheels they can be either two or three. They is the mechanism used to keep the blade to its place. Also, there's the support framework that could be made up of a table or a bench that should be strong and durable enough for day-to-day working. Bandsaws are available in various sizes, ranging from the stand-alone tables to floor models.

These types of benchtops are easy to move around, and can be placed on a level surface or placed firmly on a suitable area to provide some assistance. They don't have the powerful capabilities of floor models, but they're much less expensive to purchase. The dimension of the bandsaw is a significant factor in determining how big a project which you're able to take on. There are two major measurements: the length between the throat of the saw and the edge of the blade's inner the tip. This is one type of measurement. e.g. If there's a space of fourteen inches between these two points, it will be able to take on lengths ranging from 10 and 24 inches. Another type of measurement is the thickness of cut created by the saw. If the blade cuts up to six inches, the typical cut is 5 to 8 inches using the identical blade.

Apart from the attributes previously mentioned, the kind of blade as well as the dimensions of the table is crucial. smaller tables will not give the space for moving the blade easily. Angle 45deg is the most common angle that is used for work in a wide table, you'll have the ability to get this accomplished, specifically in conjunction with the lathe. There is an miter gauge to aid in cutting crosscuts and the fence allows the resawing of your bandsaw.

Band saws are also equipped with the ability to adjust tension according to the length of blade's tension.

The guides for the blade can be rotated upwards and downwards so that it matches the material's durability or toughness. is broken down.

Resawing is among the most challenging sawing processes and involves cutting hard wood into a smaller stock. Sometimes, this is used to cut the wood has a high figure is chosen for door panels or a cabinet projects. Large blades are required. The rules for the use of the saw should be adhered to correctly to keep the blade from drifting away or "running out." Also, a fence needs to be put in place. However, despite all this, errors are likely to happen; the saw blade can be prone to cutting across the board from one side to the other. In this case, for instance an example, a Jet saw is equipped with a resaw guide, which gets fixated to the fence and reduces or eliminates the problem of leading. High fences can be made from wood stock, and then attached with the table.

SCARF DOVETAIL CONSTRUCTION

Chapter 7: Straight-Line Joints

Rubbed joint

them as spring joints can be very effective in connecting two edges of a board for a complete panel. they're a disaster for those with non tightened rubbed joints.

The most attention has been placed on sprung joints. many works have been written and published highlighting the joint's benefits. Though I am in agreement with their claims however, sometimes things that are obvious tend to be lost. The way we apply a kind of method which is drilled into our minds by an insidious claim based on others' opinions that could lead to catastrophic results when we made the use of similar techniques however, this time with an entirely different approach. These limitations should not be ignored, but incorporated when future endeavors are that are to be undertaken.

The success of a rubbed joint is comprised of two essential elements an adhesive as well as two straight, unbroken edges. The sprung joint has an additional hollow in the middle. This is why creating perfect rubbed joints would be difficult. A second point is that the type of adhesive that is best for joint rubbing is called hide glue. Sure, you can get rid of small parts using PVA, or another fast-setting glues, however for small cabinets or table, or perhaps for a table with a coffee maker, one type of glue known as the hide glue will be fit the bill for this kind of use, i.e., rubbed joint. The hide glue can pull two joined edges when it is dried, which leads to the creation of a solid joint. In order for this to occur, there need to have no gaps.

Screw joint

The screwed butt joints make the use of screws that are inserted immediately following the joint is joined. They are usually inserted at the point of the wood or the long grain of the member, and then elongated by the joint until they reach the member's end grain. Because of this that long screws are required to ensure that traction. The joints can undergo jointery but it's not required however.

When working with solid timber the norm is to drill a hole into the frame. This can be done in order to conceal the head of the screw. This allows for a bigger section of the screw's body to enter the component for more the traction. Once the screw is inserted in the joints, the counterbore may be filled using a medium and sized dowel that is an offcut of the same wood. This is done by using cutting tools for the plug.

There are a variety of systems made available for the screwed butt joints There's a provision for caps made of plastic that can be secured on the screw head once it has been driven back into. Counterbores aren't required in these fasteners. This method of operation is unique to produced products made of board.

This type of joint can be found on both the carcase as well as frame joinery. Modular kitchens make good recourse to this fix method.

The various uses for screw joints can be found in:

Joinery for frames (e.g. frame joinery, face frames web frames doors frames)

Cabinet carcase building (carcase sides to top and bottom, fixed shelving/partitions).

Spline joints

A spline join is created when a spline made of wood is introduced and firmly bonded into a slot that's been cut at another woodworking joint typically a mitered or butt joint.

The spline will be put into place to strengthen the joint, and aid in keeping the section's alignment with each the other. This tiny addition provides a great deal of power to the joint is being used.

Spline can be made from wood, plywood or similar materials. the joint being strengthened. To ensure durability natural woods, the grain of woods must be arranged to run through the joint within the working piece.

It is not recommended to force splines into grooves that can cause splitting or distortion. Instead, they must be able to slide into the grooves with no stress and without other play in order to allow for the adhesive to create solid joints.

When used between two boards, such as edge or miter joints and The length of the spline ought to be slightly smaller than both slots to make sure the joint is sealed.

Miter spline

Miter spline are useful for strengthening picture frames, and also frame frames for cabinet faces that have mitered corners. Small decorative boxes may make use of various colored splines and edge mitering to give visual impact as well as reinforcement for joining.

Miter spline joint designs are stunning with different wood shades. The bright spline placed in a dark wood can bring out the joint. A spline of dark walnut placed in lighter wood will likely to do similarly.

Edge Spline

Splines can be utilized to make larger and more expansive panels from numerous smaller boards. A glue that is edge-to-edge up is strong because of its lengthy grain-to-long grain surface; splines offer additional support and also aid to align the joint.

The most well-known edge spline joint features the groove, and spline which runs across the entire length of boards. The spline can be seen when you view the joint at the ends.

If aesthetics aren't important, plywood can be the ideal spline choice for this task. The spline is derived from the hardwood to provide striking contrast.

The spline that is halted the same as a halted dado joint because the groove is stopped just short of the end of the board however, this occurs on both sides in this case.

These are used for the edges of wood furniture such as tables. The woodworker may require more strength through the spline but when there is no sightlines.

While the groove could be made using the table saw, it's likely to be easier and quicker to cut it using a router table and the slotting bits.

The corner of the slot could undergo the process of chiseling into an equilateral triangle that can accept the spline. its edges can be smoothed to create a perfect circular shape with the Sander.

edge joint

The art of creating a flawless edge joint is an essential project for cabinet makers aware that boards are available in small sizes these days.

In the ideal world in a perfect world, if the 36" broad cherry board is required for the edge of your dining table, you might visit the lumberyard and choose from a stack of 36" broad cherry boards. They are all created from trees measuring 60"-70" in the diameter. However, in the present world there is a chance that you can want to request a yardhand from the nearest lumberyard and they have 36" wide cherry boardsyou can only guess at the answer you will receive.

A few years ago, when I needed 18" broad cherry boards to give Queen Anne highboy, I encountered difficulties trying to find nice 10" boards which could be easily glued together in two. We often are glued up to boards with a measurement of 8-10" from tiny stock. This depicts adequately the constantly changing nature of hardwood in American forests. Rather than taking mature trees with diameters of approximately 40" or greater as the predecessors did out, a lot of woodworkers make use of smaller pieces. The result is an edge joint. This makes it one of the top joint for any cabinet maker.

Edge joints can be connected with splines that are cross-grained or biscuit joints. They aid in alignment, however they also provide some durability and an adequate amount of surface. Edge joints are sometimes created using the tongue-and-groove style of cutting. The technique is often used in joints that aren't connected, such as when you're butting materials for flooring or cabinets.

The cabinetmaker uses the basic butt joint, which is glued to the other with very strong glue. If they're constructed, butt joint is extremely strong, often larger and heavier than the lumber that lies close to joining.

The joint is constructed with the help of a machine

One of the simplest things that you can do to ease your edge joints' state is to get access to the tables in your jointer to make sure they are aligned properly. The infeed table's width should be reduced until its top is one eighth" lower than the table above. Lay a wide straight edge along both tables. Its bottom edge should depend on the surface of the table above and sit 1/8" higher than the table below. of the table beneath.

Perform a thorough test for an unchanging one-quarter" gap between the straight edge base and infeed table's surface across its total length. You should also do a proper check to ensure that there is a constant 1/8" gap along the entire length of your table. If any changes are discovered, you must go through the manual of the user for specific instructions on how to resolve the problem.

This type of inspection should only be conducted at least once per year. It is however recommended that you perform this type of check with an Try Square to experience that the fence line is at 90 degrees away from tables.

Before an edge is joined, you need to establish a planar reference to a similar surface on the board which is going to be joined. In the minimum, one part of the board to be joined must be leveled. The process can be performed by your joinery machine, provided that its cutting head is wide enough. If not then you can consider flattening the reference plane put on the board using hand planes as well as some winding sticks. You can also do my routine with large boards: split them into two pieces to join with the other half having been sanded and aligned using my 6-inch" jointer.

Unfortunately, it isn't possible to do any straightening on the board with the thickness planer due to the small dimensions of this table. This device makes a certain part of the board look smooth and guarantees parallelism with the opposite surface. If the reference surface moves frequently, the thickness planner can ensure that the surface's smoothness, while securing the squeaks.

Because you are able to edge join an item that has only one flattened face (the one you'll put into the fence) Two straight, smooth, adjacent surfaces offers more possibilities in transferring stock to the jointer. Therefore, I highly recommend flattening opposite sides of the thickness planeer. There is no requirement in this stage to get the boards down until the thickness that you want to achieve.

Chapter 8: Machined Joints

Scarf joints

Scarf joints have been used for the building of wooden vessels for a long time. There are a myriad of variations to this type of joint; some variants include tabbed, feathered and hooked scarfs. There are a variety of uses that can be made of them, from connecting plansks together to making that is the lengthiest staves using very small pieces.

The advancement in engineering for structural construction, which led to lighter vessels, and also significant advances in glues, the characteristics and capacities when they are compared to or paired with hardwood lumber must be understood.

The scarves' description is based on the amount of slopes around the piece's hardness that are paired to form a relationship. This is referred to as an easy ratio.

Below are a few instances of the application of a scarf joint;

Bevel-cut scarves

If you break the edges of angles the angle is exposed to longer grain to create stronger bonds. The less rounded the angle, the greater and stronger the surface for gluing. A 45deg bevel increases the value of the gluing surface by forty percent, and helps hide the joint lines on an attractively cut surface. For a perfect alignment with the angles, cut one side on the other of the blade. Then, cut the end that is mating in the opposite part. If the bevel angle on your saw blade is different from 45deg, both parts will remain being mated.

Miter-cut scarves

Use this joint to make a larger and more wide the surface for gluing. Create the 4:1 angle guide which is greater than the width of the pieces. Similar cleats at both ends of the triangle assist in positioning across the surface of the two pieces. The angles of the two workpieces should be noted and the pieces bandsawed until they are within 1/32" of the lines of scrap sides.

A slip joint an enormous smooth, machine-cut joint to do small batch jobs such as the edges of wooden frames. It has the same fundamental geometry in its surface or face as a conventional Bridle joint, however, it's constructed in an extremely unique manner.

The slim, large proportions are able to offer a vast area for gluing.

Slip joint

By using the bandsaw, and a bit of preparation, the possibility of creating a variety of identical slip joints becomes an option for anyone. When a joint is perfectly fitted then everything else becomes simple.

The most common use for the slip joint is to frames with corners that are low profile. Frames need sturdy wood that won't twist and bow if there's any change in the water content. It is possible to prepare the wood by using simple hand tools or equipment, If you're using the power of an electronic planning device you should round it off using a hand plane immediately after. Utilize the grain in order to remove any ridges that may appear across the surfaces.

You should be prepared to test some speculation at first the key to making properly-fitted slip joints lies on the side of shims' elasticity. When the shims are maintained in the same condition and each joint you use afterwards will perfectly.

Joints made of biscuits This is a butt-joint that's reinforced which has an oval shape. The biscuit is constructed of solid and dried wood similar to the beech used in two pieces of timber that are matched to mortises and Tenons. Most people make use of biscuit joiners for making matching mortises in instances where accuracy is not essential. The joint was designed to allow for flexibility when glue is applied.

Scribed joint

The joint that is ascribed in use when two distinct mouldings join at the interior corner. In lieu of being mitered the edge of a piece is shaped to match into the contour of the adjacent piece. The scribed joint can also be considered to be coping joints and coping saws have been developed to serve this function. This type of joint is when you are the installation of skirting boards. For instance, it's best option to have the scribed joint on all angle of corrosion inside and a different kind of joint, called the miter joint to deal with external angles. It is due to the fact that wood may shrink as it gets wider, making the miter joints open to the inside. This would not be a good thing.

Special joint

Chinese chair Joint

Chinese furniture was present for a lengthy duration. Lacquer furniture was present in Han dynasty's tombs in the beginning of around 206 B.C. and during the Southern and Northern Dynasties from (420-589) and under the influence of Buddhists as well as the influence of the Buddhists Chinese began to adopt the custom of sitting on platform-like platforms and seated with feet inclined on furniture such as the stool and chairs.

It is a luxurious mortise and tenon method and its durability smoothness, seamlessness, and sturdy creation of joints made from wood. It is, however, a fashionable and elegant method, it's longevity is reasons that a large number of woodworkers are still using this technique to the present. It's not new. Chinese Architects have put mortise and tenon joinery in home construction as well as other woodwork for many years. It is for this reason that this type of joinery was used even to the present mostly due to its durability and accessibility to building. With no material for fixing, the durability is constant over the life of.

Indeed, although it is true that a variety of Chinese dynasties have gone through implementation and spread a wide range of ideas regarding building designs, Chinese joinery is still unchanging. It's been tested as a method and is a popular label to cabinetmakers. Therefore, when furniture from China is offered to you the strength and durability is evident. Mortise and tenon techniques are highly regarded in China due to its rarity and straightforward type of joinery.

cornice joint

Coving, cornice and architrave are words commonly used in incorrectly or as if they are identical.

A cornice can be described as a moulding that is used to cover the gap that connects a ceiling to walls, which guarantees that it won't need to be finished. It also ensures that any cracks or irregularities can be covered.

Cornices can be simple or elaborately crafted.

Plain cornice is sometimes referred to as "coving.'

Coving and cornice are made of plaster made of paper, a polyurethane-covered, and paper-covered as well as a variety of others.

An architrave can be described as a type of moulding that is placed over a window, door or another type of opening. In this particular instance it extends from the sides of the molding up to the opening. The term "architrave" is used to refer to or refer to any horizontal or upright moldings which form the structure of windows, doors, or any other openings within the industry of building. The term architrave can be derived from wood.

Green woodworking joint

A different type of woodcraft is Green woodworking, or more precisely, carpentry. This is about turning green or unseasoned timber into the form of finished furniture. Unseasoned wood refers to a kind that is just removed or conserved by keeping the wood in a trough that is filled with water to ensure its higher volume of water. The green wood is less brittle than seasoned timber which makes it much simpler to work with hand equipment. Since the wood isn't seasoned, it has lost its moisture content shrinkage takes place as well, and green woodworkers could use the shrinkage to determine very secure joints within their work. In order to increase the effect of shrinkage the one side of the joint could be dried out in an oven while the second part is left in to turn green. The parts tighten each other as they switch moisture to the surroundings. The expansion of the Tenon in the growing "green" mortise creates a extremely strong, secure permanently bonded joint, even when adhesives aren't offered. A different traditional green woodworking task is bodging.

Chapter 9: The Craft Of Joinery Demands

That must develop over years. Joinery, an aspect of woodworking, involves the joining of well-crafted wood pieces together to create beautiful and stunning wood craft. It is possible to create wood joints with bindings adhesives or the appropriate sort of glue. They have distinctive features like their look as well as their flexibility, strength and durability. It is because of the specific materials employed and the role each joint plays in. In order to satisfy the demands of woodworkers everywhere There are a variety of alternatives for joinery. For each piece of furniture is likely to vary from one piece to the next.

That is exactly what you need for the construction of the construction.

While two pieces of wood are joined with the use of nails or screws it will not offer the same strength and aesthetics of a carefully made piece of artwork. Furniture with joints provides enormous value and gives an elation for the person who owns it and the woodworker.

There are a variety of joints and each kind has its own function. Knowing how joints function is essential. Joinery made of wood can be classified into two categories: those which don't require any fasteners (the traditional technique) as well as those with fasteners. Non-traditional techniques are made up of domino and biscuit joint. joints, which improve the stability and look of joints with simpleness and elegance.

Traditional wood joinery makes use of the wood's natural properties to cut down on the cost of external components. This kind of joinery was modified through times based upon regional customs and the place which regions it is the most frequently utilized. There are many joints used throughout Asia as well as in the Middle East without nails or glue. The materials can have a negative impact on the earth and are not suited to any function . They also have large amounts of resin, which do not work with glue .

The strength of your joints indicates that your woodwork is excellent. To cut precisely it is necessary use a jig along with fencing. The fence and jig are indispensable tools used in woodworking. Jigs can be utilized to aid in dissection. Other instruments that could need to be used include router bits and saw blades. Fence is the term for the rigid flat tip of a power saw which can be utilized to hold the piece of material cutting .

Every wood is distinctive . Woods could be described as similar to humans but possessing unique particularities that allow them to distinct. These features are what make the woods that are unique, and why they are designated . This is something you should take into consideration when picking timber for woodworking project . The density and composition of the wood determines which class they belong to . It is crucial to

For the best result To achieve your desired outcome, first you need to know the properties of wood.

Hardwood with an engineered softwood

Softwoods

Lumber and timber are two kinds of softwood that are made from conifer tree. Gymnosperms is the scientific name for conifers. They reproduce cones and feature similar features to needles. Cedar, Fir, and Redwood are just a few of the softwood trees used for cabinetmaking, woodworking and in other crafts .

Hardwoods

The term "hardwood" refers to any tree which produces needles and neithes as well as cones made from softwoods. Angiosperms is another term used to describe hardwoods. Deciduous trees may also be named angiosperms . Hardwoods are able to produce seeds and leaves.

There are a variety of hardwoods such as oak the maple, cherry, and mahogany. While hardwoods may not be as sturdy than softwoods, they are renowned for their stunning and distinctive pattern of wood grains.

Though some species of wood can be classified as hardwoods, they are not deciduous as the bamboo or palm . They are scientifically known as monocotyledons. They are akin to hardwoods, and are often called

hardwoods. Engineered wood isn't often utilized to distinguish bamboo from palm.

Engineered wood

Engineered woods are the final sort you'll discover . They are typically produced because they can't be discovered in the natural environmental conditions .

Wood treated with engineering can be treated by heating or chemicals

processes. The purpose of this is to produce a unique wood item that can be made to meet the requirements of certain dimensions, and also has distinctive characteristics that nature is unable to give.

Plywood is one of the examples of engineered wood . Wood veneers may be regarded as engineered wood due to the nature they are manipulated . It is an activity that must occur on occasions.

Moisture Content and Movemen t

Wood is able to expand and contract that can seem surprising when you consider how much movement is involved in the piece . If you are embarking on a project It is essential to think about the motion. Wood moves as the water content of it is altered. The wood of a tree is green after being removed. The sap fills in the gaps . The sap is responsible 72 percent of the total water content in wood, though the percentage of sap can differ depending on the type of wood. The wood fibers account for the remainder of 28% and are able to penetrate the cell walls of wood. The sponge grows in size in the event of wetness. Wood fibers have the same result when they are placed in humidity conditions .

The wood will begin drying immediately following drying. After the wood is dried it will be able to absorb water or moisture evaporates . The wood's shape and size remain the same until the point at which water is released. Following that, expansion occurs .

Following evaporation, about from 4%-11% remains within the wood. Wood's moisture content can be determined by the environmental conditions . The amount of water that wood contains can be affected by the amount of water that is present in the surroundings. Both of them are directly proportional. In other words, the increase of one variable is accompanied by an increase of the other . Wood is lost about 1% per 5 % increase in humidity .

The size of wood fiber increases as is moist. In the event that water evaporates, wood fiber decreases . It causes expansion of wood and shrinkage . In the northern hemisphere there's a shift in humidity from winter to the summer season. The relative humidity in the indoors as well as outdoors is greatly influenced through fireplaces or air conditioning . If temperatures inside are distinct, the humidity may differ from one structure to the next . Woods' longevity can be affected by fluctuations in the weather and season.

Direction of Movemen t

Wood grows and shrinks continuously in a steady fashion . The movement of wood across all directions isn't particular. The design of the grain permits it .

Three directions can be considered .

The grain of the wood is in line with its stability along the length of its length . The dimension of green lumber is reduced to 0.1 percent after drying. The length of a longboard is 8 feet. 332 inches of motion . The wood movement along the lines of the grain is connected to the growth. That means approximately 8 percent length loss can be accomplished when you travel in that direction.

Aproximately 4% of diameter of the tree is extending along the radial axis and starts at the pith. The quarter sawn wood is much more durable than plain-sawn lumber due to reasons that are mentioned earlier . Plain sawn lumber is susceptible to dissection tangential . This causes the lumber to be twice as swift than quarter-sawn lumber exposed to radial dissection. The tangential motion to one side is around 8percent, while the radial movement on the other is about 4percent .

Chapter 10: Hand Tool

Tool types are those which can be operated with a hand and don't require power. They are more akin to an actual tool. They include hammers and cutters, as well as clamps.

Hand Tool Hand-tools are necessary for everyday tasks. The types of jobs which require hand tools are gardening, woodworking among others.

Hand tools are plentiful and that are available for use in general, and also high-quality brand names. Hand tools have become an essential element in most households as well as workshops.

Here are a few general-purpose hand instruments:

Knives

There's no way to define kitchen knives in this way . The best knife is found in every tool kit. It is a tool to be used for crafting. They are constructed of solid materials that could be used to break unblock boxes, letters and other items as well as cut through less difficult substances. Be sure that the knife the lade is secured when it's is not being used for security reasons.

Scissors

To serve a variety of purposes There is the scissor within almost every home. It is useful in nearly every situation that requires cutting for example, projects at school and in the kitchen. They can also be used for DIY tasks or other situations where they are required . It can also be used to open seals or packaging.

Screwdrivers

There are many dimensions and designs of this device . This is the most common tool in homes . Screwdrivers are utilized to connect screws to hinges and fix them to surfaces. It is also possible to use them for mounting lamp holders and lighting switches within cabinet design . There are a variety of screwdriver blades that are available and each has a unique size to suit the purpose . Carbon steel that is used to fabricate the blade is treated to improve the durability . In order to ensure that the handle is secure the handle could be constructed from a specific plastic .

Hammers

The tool has the capacity to apply large quantities of force over only a certain area . The tool

It is made up of a wood stick as well as a block of metal . It's used to fix nails, breaking items into smaller pieces as well as forging metal. It should not weigh too much so that it exerts all its force when connecting nails to the wall . To make it easy to lift and handling the hammer should be the proper dimension to hold the person who uses it.

Wrench

Wrenches help to hold objects and then turn the objects . They can be used to fix wooden work to bicycles or unlock bolts or nuts in order to fix them. Hand tool manufacturers create various wrenches that accommodate the needs of woodworkers .

Pliers

They are commonly used throughout homes . These tools can be useful in keeping objects firmly in place by removing screws and bolts as well as bending certain material . It straightens, bends and even cuts wires . The most effective type of pliers is one that cuts wires, and also has needle-nose tips. The pliers are used either at home or at workshops .

Clamps

This tool is utilized to join objects to stop them from moving or moving apart by the use of an inward motion . These hand tools may be temporary as they can be used to help hold wooden pieces in their place when they're being used. But, they could also be permanently. They are most frequently for repairing or assembling wooden structures or to complete other DIY tasks .

Chisel

One of the most popular tools that has been used in the history of woodworking includes the chisel . Chisels are tools equipped with a stainless steel blade connected to pickets, or a handle made of plastic. It is employed alongside mallets or hammers for cutting the wood, break it up, or pare wood . Chisels are typically utilized to create and shape woodwork joints .

Paring cuts are usually made using chisels in order to smooth the surface of the wood. When cutting is utilized as a technique, it is used to eliminate wood levels piece one at a time . It is possible to use hand pressure to take the wood. You can also make use of a cutting machine to slice large pieces .

Mallets that are intentionally struck as well as chisel and hammer. This is normally determined by the extent to which the chisel's hammer penetrates into the wood. The angle that the blade is in contact with the surface of the wood can be changed to change the angle .

To cut wood it is essential to be sure of the pressure that is applied to your hands. Every hand must be utilized for holding the knife . The dominant hand should rest placed on the handle. The other hand should be wrapped over the blade, or push it. Press the chisel against the wood using a slicing motion . Split cutting is another application of the cutting chisel . You can place it where you'll need to cut the grain on the tips of your wood. Use mallets to smash the handle. For the wood to be separated into pieces, you can move the chisel in fibres or along the grain. This is a method that can be extremely efficient for quickly eliminating large volumes of material. However, the method is constrained by the grain's direction in the event that it's not straight, or even to your advantage .

Straight cuts can be made into the grain using cutting and chopping however this isn't necessarily possible . It is possible to use this method to create mortises and other recesses. If your chisel isn't capable of piercing the wood by using a hammer then you may want to consider placing the chisel at a different angle . This is a great method to use by removing portions of wood in a slow manner .

There are many different kinds of Chisels

There are a variety of Chisels . Bevel-edged ones are most well-known. These are best suited to carpentry using tools. But, if you've got one of them types, they are able to be utilized in other ways, however they are not as flexible. Firmer chisel Butt chisels Mortise.

Power Tools

These devices or machines can be powered by humans by utilizing another source of power. They include pneumatics and internal combustion engines, and internal combustion engines with electrical motors.

Power tools are only to be employed in certain environments environment. It is crucial to ensure that the device you buy performs specific tasks and is able to be safely used in specific situations .

The various types of power tools and their uses the Air Compressor

This powerful device is built on the fundamental premise. It transforms the power that is stored in an air compressor into necessary energy to perform the work. It works by holding air until it is at its capacity. The capacity of the compressor can differ based on the type of compressor you select.

The type of tool can be used to spray paint, for house and workshop clean-up, filling cars tires and making gas cylinders for cooking . Additionally, it can be used to charge a variety of pneumatic devices including nail guns as well as different kinds of the hammers .

Trimmer

A quality trimming tool is all you require to make your garden an attractive and appealing landscape . Instead of the standard blade, trimmers utilize monofilament lines, which are employed to slice grass . It allows for cutting grass, as well as other things and also deal with uneven surfaces. Though a trimmer's motor is powered by gasoline, today there are electric motor trimmers in the market . It is utilized for cutting grass. It gives plants attractive structure and looks in cutting out uneven sections of the land . It is also possible to use the trimming machine for various farming needs .

Table Saw

Table saws are handy tool that can be used to cut cuts and cutting any kind of materials. The table saw comes with a sawing mechanism under the table which permits users to swiftly move the materials you put onto it. The table saw is driven by an electric motor and is able to be moved from the site of work due to its transportation feature . The table saw is perfect for cutting deep, which is not possible using other power saws.

Drill

Most likely, this is the helpful tool at house . There are numerous kinds of drills available to be used in many different jobs. The drill is able to help with a myriad of tasks. You can use it to hang paintings as well as to make furniture or make the work of a metal .

Chapter 11: Simple Joinery

Simple joinery is an incredibly well-known method for joining woods together. The discussion will focus on the following subjects :

Wood grain, strength and hardness

Technically speaking, the term "grain" refers to the direction of fibres in wood. This differs from the picture. This is a reference to the distinctive pattern that is a result of different grain positions. It can be either a blessing or a curse for all grain types with the exception of straight grain. For wood to have a grain that is different from straight, the grain can be sliced to create an appealing shape. The irregular grain could serve as a benefit. In terms of structural use like home construction wood with straight grain is weaker. Wooden boards with straight grain requires more attention in machining, to prevent damage and unwanted reaction.

What exactly is it that is so vital about woodworking ?

Natural wood is an element. It's more durable when the grain is constant. Wood could be an organic or chemical compound . It's composed of multiple strands or polyose fibers that are joined by the use of polymer binder . Imagine stacking a lot of straws and stacking them into a linear way . When one straw has a weak point, the other straws can add strength to the pile . If you cut wood across the grain, you're breaking the bonds of polymer (easy). If you cut along the grain, you'll produce polyose fibres, which have a much longer lifespan .

Pay attention to the grain's direction for the best benefit the strength of wood. For you to make sure that the fibers flow freely across the grain, you must orient your body constantly .

Assist the burden

As much as possible, be sure you can ensure that the grain runs along the entire length of the boards.

Simple joinery Dado can be an efficient and effective method to connect two standard pieces. They are very useful for building bookshelves and cabinets.

Dados are cuts in the wood to serve as a reference for a different piece. If you want to build a shelf from the thickness of 3/4 inches then you'll need to make an opening that is 3/4 inch wide and then attach the shelf the groove.

Techniques for Cutting Dados

There are a variety of ways to design a fathero . A common technique for creating a dado is to place a stackable dado cutter on a table mounted saw. They include a pair of 10-" size, one-eighth" kerf sawblades, and a few 1/16 one-inch or 1/8 chippers . The user can either use chippers or add them to create any width groove that is between

1/4" to 3/4 1' . When you make multiple passes with the saw, it is possible to cut dadoes with bigger diameters . A dado cutter stacked is also known as a dado cutter can only use on table saw, or on circular armsaws. This type of dado should not be utilized on circular saws. It could be the risk of injury to you .

The wobble dado can be considered an alternative for that of the stack set . It is essentially an edged saw mounted on a rotating wheel . The width of the dado is adjustable by changing the direction of the blade in the spindle. The dado is cheaper than the one that is stacked . The results from this set can be uncertain and do not depend upon my prediction.

These are very rare and therefore are not considered acceptable .

It is my goal to stay clear of buying an unbalanced dado. Instead, I pay to buy the one that is stacked. I'm not sure about the risk of the wobbler set.

A Router for Cutting Dadoe s

Utilizing a router's aligned and dissecting tool is an established way to cut dadoes . There may be a need to reduce the speed of your router in order to break down the dado.

To monitor the guide to ensure that you have a perfectly aligned border. It ensures that the cut is straight. The 3/4" router bit will be used to dissect a dado that is slightly larger than a 3/4 inch plywood sheet . Even though 23/32 bits are readily available, a 1/2" bit along with two passes are enough to provide the results you desire.

Edge joint

The most common joint type is the edge-to-edge joint . The edge to edge joint can be used for joining table tops of differing lengths but with the same in thickness. For this it is used to join biscuits to join the edges of the boards . If you are planning to mix tabletops made from pieces of wood from various companies put them side-by-side in which the boards' grain is in the opposite direction . This helps to maintain the stability of your table when it expands and contracts .

When the joints are located in the right place You can then draw with a pencil marks every 4 to 6". These would represent the lines that run through the biscuit slots.

The next step is for the board to be separated . The size of a large number 20 is most commonly used when it comes to this .

Set the fence of the guide directly on the top of the stock. Be sure that the marks you've made by a pencil align to the cutting guide . Secure the fence and begin to cut. After the motor has reached maximal speed, you can slide the blade down the wood until it is difficult to slide into the wood. After that, you can remove the complete blade. Continue the process on the pencil's next line .

After every slot has been removed, it is time to apply some adhesive to each edge. Apply a bit of glue to join the pieces together . You can attach every corner of the tabletop fast and join the parts. Make sure the clamps are secured so that every space is sealed . Be careful not to squeeze the clamps too much in order to stop the glue from spilling . In order to avoid messy finishes Clean up any spills of glue quickly .

Coopered Joints

There are a variety of kinds and sizes of containers with staves, from wooden barrels to firkins with barrels between . Coopers are the biggest plane. Coopers boast a 6-foot jotter facing toward the sky. The wood's one end is put on the floor with the opposite end is supported by two legs. The Cooper procedure is a method of holding each stave with precisely the bevels. If the procedure repeats on the following stave, it forms the cask to be large.

Each stave is created of the identical angles. The angle of each stave can be 90°. The Cooper drawknive is a contoured shape for the stave prior to moving it towards an jointer . The stave's back appears like an elongated circle. Every edge is precisely aligned to the circle's 90-degree angle. This unique stave is constructed no matter the size of the stave. It's possible to see exactly the correct angle near the point of the circle regardless of dimensions . For a perfect result, this procedure should be repeated several times .

Materials such as porch columns and circular tips to chests are covered works for which joiners are responsible for . Joiners operate in the same way as coopers. Beginning with the stock. Eggs need to be beveled, with adhesives glued to the surface

. Each edge should be equal to the angles between face stock .

Create a drawing of a complete size on the paper. Next, you need to determine the angles by drawing. If you would rather be more scientific, divide the circle in angles of 360, using the number of staves as you like .

Each stave is 45 degrees. The eight staves give an total of eight. The angle inside is what we're looking for. However, after subtracting 45 degrees, 180 degrees becomes 135 degrees. Half of 135 is equal to 67.5

Degrees. The circle forms when 8 equal-length staves join together using edges with underbevelin G of 67.5deg. Once the angles are established, it is necessary to place them exactly at the edge . The square is 90 degree angle. But the bevel that slides can be secured at any angle that you'd like . It is recommended to set the angle to 54 degrees for the five-sided item. The edges are scrutinized as the planes are cut . Make sure that each starve has the same length. If the angles aren't extreme, you can't proceed with the plan. The excess is often thrown away due to the lack of clarity on which direction to take .

Rabbet

Another type that is popular is the"rabbet. It is used to cut board edges more than at its core . It's often employed to join edges so that they are firmly joined .

Interlocking siding or wainscoting could be employed in the in the past. If you do, you'll know an tongue and groove joint. The wood joint is utilized for keeping boards together on their edges, not between their edges. One particular edge is bent using an

This is known as the tongue. It's the portion that protrudes and the groove the recess. They're tightly joined .

The glues must be utilized for holding the joint in place . The grove and tongue should be cut with an acute angle. To make sure it stays on the same plane the woo dworks and angles must be merged . It is simpler if you are equipped with the correct router bits . The process can be executed with the aid of hand-planners . The term groove refers to a cut or trench cut out of woodwork. It's aligned along the grain. Grooves differ from a dagger because dados are positioned across the grain, whereas it aligns itself with the grain . Grooves are used in cabinet making and different woodworking fields for a variety of uses.

Chapter 12: The Mortise And Ten On Join

Over the years woodworkers have utilized this type of joint in their works. Particularly in cases where the angles of joints are greater than 90 degrees They're simple and durable in their basic form however they are flexible enough to fulfill a variety of functions . A tenon tongue is by far the most commonly used mortise, or tenon . The tenon is generally the extension of a rail, and then cut into the exact shape of a wood item, is made by hand . In order to ensure that the tenon is precisely in the mortise the tenon should be fitted with be erroneous. Apart from the shoulders there are other materials or methods to fix the joint. This includes pins and wedges, glue, and pins . The type of joint is utilized by blacksmiths in addition to woodwork and carpentry .

Stonemasons

Below are a few other mortise types could be used in your work.

Half-dovetail mortise: It has a greater rear surface of the area than that on the front. It is filled with wedges which means that the wedge can't be taken out . Stub Mortise This mortise has less depth that other mortise types. It's not able to go through the piece of wood and is only able to travel to a specific distance.

Through mortise: here, the mortise completely runs through the piece of wood.

Open mortise This is in the uppermost part of the timber and typically is constructed with three sides .

Blind mortise: the tenon has been fully inserted into the mortise and is not visible. It's used for the design of tables and chairs.

Tenons can be bonded to pieces of wood by stretching their length into mortises. Tenons typically are longer than the width they cover . There are various kinds of Tenons.

Through Tenon. The hole is passed through and can be clearly seen on the opposite side.

Biscuit Tenon It comes as a biscuit .

A loose tenon is a kind of tenon doesn't join to the wood parts that are to be joined It can employed without regard to the connection . Tusk Tenon. This is a kind of wedge device is utilized to hold the joint in place.

Pegged Tenon. Pins and pegs are put into the hole in the mortise or Tenon.

Stub Tenon. The diameter of the hole is determined by the volume of wood utilized. Additionally, the mortise is an extra wide width than the Tenon, to avoid the tenon being visible .

It's a good idea to ensure that the dimension of your mortise as well as Tenon in proportion to the size of the wood . It's an excellent method of woodcrafting to be sure that the length of the Tenon is around 30 percent.

MORTISE and TENON EXERCIS E

It is possible to make mortise, tenon or even a tenon by using an abrasive table. Follow the instructions.

Cut the board of wood to the size you require. Be sure that the edge of the wood that is used for cutting the tenon for the mortise is completely straight. Utilize the Try Square to mark the length of the piece of wood to be used in the mortise .

Three-quarters of an inch between the top of the t-op as well as the top of the marks made at step 2. make three-quarters marks. This is your starting and ending point for the mortise.

Note the mortise boards at each end by measuring 1/3 of their thickness. This will determine the width of the mortise .

Begin by placing the longest straight tooth onto the router. Then, you cut the router in order to make the mortise. Take note of the stop and start places in the first section . Start slow, starting by using the smallest tooth. Then, slowly increasing the depth until you have reached a 1 inch mortise.

The tenon's mark is one-third of its thickness. After that, the wood is moved slowly across the quarter-inch router teeth on the other side, until it is one-inch deep. Turn the wood around and repeat the procedure for the opposite side .

Make sure you are in good shape and make any necessary adjustments .

NOTE:

This measurement applies to an extremely thin block of wood . The measurements can be varied according to the thickness of your block and also the size of the weight that you wish your joint to bear .

The mortise first with a hack to mortise construction or the tenon construction

A tenon needs to be constructed prior to being fitted to the mortise. But, a mortise can't be resized to accommodate the Tenon .

The Bridle Join t

There are many commonalities between the mortise, the tenon, and the bridle joints. Tenon is divided in two places. On the other side, an mortise is made in order that the tenon will be taken in a comfortable manner . There are several glue options that could be employed to help support the joint, and keep the joint from breaking or any other unpleasant acts . For a stronger joint support, pins and screws are a good option to ensure it is in good working order .

Chapter 13: Display Joint

The Butterfly Joint

This joint is great to join boards. Also, it can be utilized to join boards which don't have proper joins . It is possible to use butterfly joints to serve as decorative, structural or other uses . The majority of the time, a butterfly joint is constructed out of a different wood than the wood used for . The butterfly joint is placed into the hole of the piece of wood. It secures the boards. Joints are utilized to keep boards in place and stop cracks from moving . Dahshur boats can be a prime example which make use of this kind of joint .

Dutch tabletops, dating back to the 18th Century and others .

Bevel top Dovetails

This type of joint is utilized in order to join various pieces by softening edges, giving a more attractive appearance as well as safety benefits. Woodworkers can benefit from this kind of joinery. of joinery can also be utilized to create relatively compact dimensions that cannot be easily changed by weather conditions.

Puzzle Scarf Joint

The perfect interlocking design is made up of two pieces. They are joined, with the proper adhesives used, and finally securely secured. The form that joins and gives the name this type of joint is very similar to the way you hold your fingers and then secure your fingers together and lock. Interlocking joints provide the most surface area to applying the adhesive, resulting in a strong and durable joint. Don't mistake a box joint with one that is a puzzle. It is used for door constructions as well as flooring boards.

DOVETAIL JOINERY

Dovetail jointing is an indication that you are a professional woodworker. The joint designs appear like fingers, are sturdy and are resistant to the rigors of. These joints don't require mechanical bolt.

It's ideal for furniture, as well as other woodwork.

A dovetail joint consists of two main components which are the tails and pins. Although the tails resemble an eagle's tail The pins and the tails are on the opposite side on the table. They try to squeeze in the center of the tail in order to form an uneasy joint to split. It is impossible to keep the joints separate if you continue adding to adhesives, and tightly joining the joints.

Dovetail joints be around for many years and can be seen in antique stores. It is easy to find dovetail joints in antique stores.

Dovetail joints have numerous benefits. It's strong, it can keep from separation, is interlocking and appealing.

Dovetail joints could have adverse consequences, such as making them difficult to cut or mark, and getting rid of all the benefits associated with them. There are various types of dovetail which can be utilized in project requirements. The choice is based on the type of project. A dovetail that is the right fit to your task will increase your abilities and showcase your capabilities.

These are the various kinds of joints that dovetail:

Dovetails with lapped edges

There are a variety of dovetail joint. Most commonly, it is the lapped dovetail. This is a method of hiding the joint on the one end but make it visible on the opposite side. The most common usage is when it comes to the design of drawers. The joint's mechanical strength is necessary to connect the sides to the side of the drawer. However, we they don't want the drawer's front view to be revealed even when the drawer is closed.

This is a difficult assembly to deconstruct. It's very similar to the dovetail through, with only the lap joint can make the debris accumulated more challenging to dispose completely out of the pin. In order to cut a laced dovetail you will require the following tools be required:

Marking gauge

Sliding bevel

Marking

template

Dovetail saw

Coping saw

Scalpel or

Scriber Bevel

Edge edge

Sliding dovetail

Woodworkers are all aware that the sliding joint is robust and dynamic when it comes to application in all aspects, from case construction up to the rail joint. Most likely, you've seen what the appearance of a sliding dovetail. It's a mix of a dado as well as a dovetail. It has a notch on one side, and one side having a tongue. side. As both wall dents are referred to as groove walls and since the side of the tongue has angles that are similar to the dovetails, joint assembly must be completed through sliding the tongue into the groove from one the other end.

The canted walls are prone to provide the sliding joint an advantage over an edging. The joint is able to resist the tension mechanically, meaning that the slat that is on the tail cannot be removed from its groove. If there are no adhesives, both parts are joined. In order to separate them it is necessary to crush the wood. crushed.

The joint's design helps in assembly tasks. It is unlikely that parts will be destroyed as you work by using clamps. Two hands are typically sufficient for assembly even in the event of multi-parts, similar to the drawer chest. Panels that have a slight bowed may be pulled into lines and without the use of fake clamping setups.

Another advantage of the dovetail that slides is that it allows components to move with out falling apart when left without glue. One example would be the breadboard's end. A thin wood strips along the edge of a board that is glued to conceal its grain at the end makes it possible to keep the panel straight. The joints are left open.

The absence of glue allows the table top to grow. Slide dovetails can be used to make extension table slides, and connect shelves to opposing side of the bookcase.

Dovetails that are blind

Dovetails that are blind, and there are:

Dovetails with half-blindness

Woodworkers typically employ a half-blind dovetail' to achieve complete obscurity of the finish grain to the side part of joinery. They are firmly inserted into mortises on the end of the board and are located on the top of the timber, concealing their edges.

Half-blind dovetails are the most commonly utilized for drawer fronts and sides. This differs in comparison to the method to attach fake doors drawers constructed with dovetails.

In the case of coupling two pieces of wood, one most commonly used joint used can be the thru dovetail. Dovetails that are through are strong as well as fascinating, but there are some instances in which this type of joint may not be the ideal.

In the case of joining of the drawer's side with the front of the drawer it is not recommended to make the use of a dovetail through joint since the ends of the tails tend to be visible through the front of the drawer.

For this situation, the best dovetail joint for use is a half-blind type of dovetail.

The half-blind or dovetail is extremely precise. As it's called, a part of this joint is able to be observed while the rest is hidden. It is not as strong similar to the dovetail through, however it is used for situations such as the front of drawers that we previously discussed.

Making half Blind Dovetails The method local to create half-blind Dovetails doesn't differ much in the method of creating through dovetails However, there are some aspects to consider:

The part that's not to be cut is known as the lap. The lap placed on the board needs to be no less than 1/8' however, it should not be able to exceed more that 1/3 pin's thickness. This is in order to ensure the dovetail's durability.

Mitred Blind Dovetail

This joint may also be known as the mitered dovetail with full blind or the dovetail with a full blind as it is utilized in the finest woodworks as well as cabinet design. The exterior portion of this joint is designed to ensure that it cannot be seen when looking at the joint. It is constructed in a way that only its interior portion that is joined at 45 degrees can be observed upon an examination. Dovetail cutting tips

1. The wood blocks should be cut to be connected to be the same size and make sure your edges are perfectly square. Make sure that they are square by using the Try square.

2. You can sand the surface you'd like with the inside facing in and mark it according to the markings. A measuring gauge could be useful.

3. The marking gauge should be set according to the thickness of the block and draw a line along those ends that you intend

to join, drawing the front and back and the two edges. It's best when the gauge is set slightly higher than the size of the block, but not more than 1/32. This creates an extension of the pins as well as ends above the block. Once it is finished and glue-up the extension allows for a bit of sanding in order to create a perfect corner.

4. Select the piece of wood that the pins will be cut out of. It is generally simpler to remove the pins before cutting them out. When deciding on the woodblock that will hold the pin, be aware that dovetail corners are able to be separated with only one edge. In order to ensure that cuts are in the pull direction. One good illustration is an drawer. The pins should be located on the block in front and the they should be on the sides. This way, you're confident that the joint will be able to hold regardless of pulling.

5. The next thing to do is find out the dimension of the pins that you plan to

employ. Pins generally are about one-third the length of tails. The size of tails can change. If you are determining tails and pins dimensions, take note of the fact the fact that long tails weaken joints. The same is true for excessively narrow tails.

6. After that, put the block of wood in an upright position and cut the end of the block with the backsaw. Follow the markings that were made earlier in step 3.

7. Make use of the chisel for cleaning off the edges of the tail to make them smooth and clean. Avoid chiseling in an instrument or a clamp; instead, place it on an even or flat surface instead.

8. Place the pins on the block of wood on which the tails will be cut. Take note of the drawn gauging line, mark the pins. The block must not shift from this stage.

9. The lines were cut and then remove the lines using a chisel, as performed in step 7 above.

10. Join the pin and tail by tapping gently to check the joint's fit. If the joint is loose, it will be difficult for the joint to remain in place. If it's too tight the joint will end up splits.

11. Once the fit has been evaluated and verified to be in good order Then glue the seams and join.

12. Smooth the edges of the joint to create a smooth surface.

A note: Two woodblocks of differing thicknesses may be joined. However, after joining it is necessary to use two measuring gauges are required that are for the thickness of the block you plan to join.

Dovetail-shaped bandsaws

Bandsaws are a useful piece of woodworking equipment employed in cutting shapes, cutting short pieces crosscut as well as the construction of cabriole legs. It is especially suited for cutting of shapes which appear irregularly formed, breaking lumber into more compact and feasible sizes, making seamless cuts, and so on.

The typical bandsaw is composed of wheels that could be one or three. These serve as the means of securing the blade's place. Additionally, there is an support frame, which may be in the shape of a table or bench that should be strong and durable enough for day-to-day working. Bandsaws can be found in different sizes, ranging from stand-alone floor models, to the tablestop models.

They are simple to transport and can be positioned on a flat surface, or placed firmly on a suitable place to offer some assistance. They aren't equipped with the strong power of the floor models, but they're much less expensive to purchase. The dimension of the bandsaw plays a major role in determining the size of project you're able to take on. There are two major kinds of measurements; the distance between the throat of the saw and the edge of the blade's inner the tip. This is an example of measurement. e.g. when there's 14 inches between these two points, the saw can manage lengths of between 10 inches and 24 inches. Another measure is the depth of cut created by the saw. If the blade is able to cut up to six inches, it is possible to cut 5 to 8 inches using the identical blade.

Alongside the functions previously mentioned, the kind of blade used and the dimensions of the table are also important. smaller tables will not give the space for moving the blade without difficulty. 45deg angle is the most common angle that is used for work on a larger table, you'll have the ability to get the job done, particularly in conjunction with lathes. There is the miter gauge that allows cutting across and also an adjustable fence to allow the resawing of your band saw. Band saws are also equipped with tension guides to correspond with the length of the blade's tension. The guides for the blade can be rotated upwards and downwards in accordance with the durability or hardness. is undergoing dissection.

Resawing is among the toughest sawing tasks and involves cutting hard wood into a smaller stock. Sometimes, this is used to cut the wood has a high-quality figured to make a door panel or cabinet design. Large blades are required. Guidelines for using the saw have to be followed correctly to keep it from wandering off or "running out." Also, a fence needs to be put in place. However, despite all this, errors are likely to happen; the saw blade can be prone to cutting between two sides. In this case, for instance an example, a Jet saw comes with an adjustable resaw guide, which gets attached to the fence of the saw and reduces or eliminates the issue of lead. High fences can be constructed from wood stock, and then attached to the table.

SCARF DOVETAIL CONSTRUCTION

Chapter 14: Straight-Line Joints

Rubbed joint

As sprung joints are excellent for gluing two edges of boards together in an entire panel, they are disastrous for rubbed joints that are not clamped. joints that are not clamped.

The most attention has been placed on sprung joints. numerous works have been published and published highlighting the joint's benefits. Although I agree with their assertion but at times, the obvious aspects tend to be lost. The way we apply a kind of method that is drilled into our minds by unsettling claims prompted by the opinions of other people that could lead to devastating results should we make the use of similar techniques and this time, an entirely different approach. These limitations should be considered and accounted for as a part of any new projects that are going being planned.

The success of a rubbed joint is comprised of just two main elements that are adhesive as well as two straight, unbroken edges. The sprung joint has an additional hollow in the middle. Without this, creating the perfect rubbed joint would not be possible. A second point is the type of adhesive that is best for joint rubbing is the hide glue. You can certainly eliminate small parts using PVA or another fastsetting glues, however to make a small cabinet, table, or perhaps for a coffee table, just one type of glue known as the hide glue is fit the bill for this kind of use, i.e., rubbed joint. The hide glue can pull two edges that are coupled when it is dried, which leads to the development of a solid joint. In order for this to occur, there need to not be any gaps.

Screw joint

The screwed butt joints make the use of screws that are inserted immediately following the joint is connected. The screws are typically inserted at the point of the wood or the long grain of the member, and then elongated by the joint until they reach the end grain of the corresponding member. Because of this that long screws are required for ensuring that excellent grip is achieved. The joints can undergo jointery but it's not required however.

When working with solid timber It is common to drill a hole into the frame. This can be done in order to conceal the screw's head. It also allows a bigger part of the body to pass through the piece for better effect. After

inserting the screw into the joint, the counterbore could be filled by a flexible and finely shaped piece of dowel made from an offcut of similar wood. This is done by making use of a saw to make the plug.

There are a variety of systems made available for the screwed butt joint There's a provision for caps made of plastic that can be secured to the screw's head after it has been driven back. Counterbores aren't required to use these kinds of fasteners. This type of fastener is the most unique feature of produced products made of board.

This type of joint can be found for both carcase as well as frame joinery. Modular kitchens make good recourse to this fix method.

A few uses for screw joints are:

Joinery for frames (e.g. Face frames door frames, web frames)

Cabinet carcase building (carcase sides to top and bottom, fixed shelving/partitions).

Spline joints

A spline joint can be made when a spline made of wood is connected and inputted to a slot which has been cut using an alternative woodworking joint that

Most of the time, it is an insertion joint or mitered.

The spline will be put on top of the joint, and aid in ensuring aligning of the sections with one the other. This tiny addition provides a great deal of force to any joint is being used.

Spline can be made from wood, plywood or other similar materials, the joint being reinforced. To ensure solidity the grain of woods that are natural is to be laid out so it is running parallel to the joint of the piece. Do not force splines to grooves that could result in splits or distortion. They should instead move in with ease and with no sides to make room for the adhesives to create an enduring connection.

When used between two boards, such as edge or miter joint and it is recommended that the length of the spline must be shorter than the two slots in order to ensure that the joint will close properly.

Miter spline

The miter spline is ideal for strengthening frame frames for pictures and frame frames for cabinet faces that have mitered corners. small decorative boxes could make use of different colored splines that have mitered edges to create visual effects as well as reinforcement for joining.

Miter spline joint designs are stunning with different wood shades. An spline with a bright hue set into dark wood can bring out the joint. A spline made of dark walnut set on a lighter colored wood will likely to do the same thing.

Edge Spline

Splines are often employed to create larger and more expansive panels from numerous smaller boards. The glue used to join edges is already strong due to its lengthy grain-to-long grains; however, splines provide additional support and also aid to align the joint.

The most well-known edge spline joint features the groove as well as a spline that runs across the entire length of boards. The spline can be seen when you view the joint at the ends.

If aesthetics aren't important, plywood can be an excellent spline to do the job. It can be made from wood to create striking contrast.

The spline with a halted edge is the same as a halted dado because the groove stops from the other end of the board however, this occurs at both ends of the case.

They're used to create the edges of furniture made from hardwood such as tables. The woodworker might want to have more power by using a spline without sightlines.

Even though the groove is made using the table saw, it's more efficient and easier to cut it using a router table and an slotting bit.

The corner of the slot could undergo shaping to create an equilateral triangle that can accept the spline. the ends can be sanded to create a perfect circular shape by using the Sander.

edge joint

A perfect edge joint is an essential job for every cabinet maker aware that boards are available in tiny sizes today.

If all things were perfect the case where the 36" broad cherry board is required for the edge of your dining table, you might visit the lumberyard and choose from a stack of 36" broad cherry boards that are all made from trees measuring 60"70" in size. However, in the present world there is a chance that you can need a yardhand at the nearest lumberyard and they have 36" wide cherry boardsyou can just imagine the reply you will receive.

A few years ago, when I was in need of 18" broad cherry boards to give Queen Anne highboy, I encountered difficulties trying to find nice 10" boards that were able to be put together together in two. We often are gluing panels that measure only 8-10" from tiny stock. This depicts adequately the constantly changing nature of hardwood in American forests. Rather than taking mature trees with diameters of approximately 40" or greater as the predecessors did out, woodworkers often make the use of smaller trees. The result is an edge joint. This makes it one of the best joint for any cabinet maker. The edge joints may be constructed using cross-grained splines or biscuit joints. They aid in alignment, but they provide durability and an adequate amount of surface. Edge joints can also be created using tongue-and groove cutting. It is sometimes used in joints that are not glue-free, like in the case of joining the floor of cabinet.

The cabinetmaker uses an ordinary butt joint that is joined to the wall using a high-quality glue. If they're constructed, butt joint are extremely strong, often more heavy and larger than the lumber that lies that is adjacent to the joint.

Making the joint using the help of machines

One of the simplest things you can do to ease your edge joints' state is accessing the jointer's tables to ensure proper alignment. Lower the height of the table infeed to a point where its top edge is one eighth" lower than the table above. Lay a wide straight edge along both tables. Its bottom edge should depend on the surface of the table above and sit 1/8" over the top of the table beneath.

Make sure you determine if there's one continuous one-quarter" gap between the straight edge base and infeed table's surface across its total length. You should also do a proper check to ensure that there is a constant 1/8" gap along the entire length of the table. If a change is discovered, you must go through the manual of the user for more information on how to resolve the issue. This type of inspection is best done every two or three years. It is also recommended that you conduct this test using the Try Square to experience that the fence has a 90deg angle away from tables.

Before a piece of edge is joined, it is necessary to make a reference plane to a similar surface on the board going to be joined. In the minimum, one portion of the board to be joined must be level. The process can be performed using your joinery equipment if the cutting head is large enough. If it's not it is recommended to attempt flattening a reference planar that is placed on your board using hand planes, and winding sticks. You can also do my routine with large boards: split them into two pieces to join with the other half having been sanded and positioned using my 6-inch" jointer.

Unfortunately, it isn't possible to carry outboard straightening by using an edge planer because of the size and shape of this table. This device makes a certain part of the board look smooth and guarantees parallelism with other surfaces. If the reference surface moves frequently, the thickness planner will guarantee the other's smoothness and minimize the rough edges.

Because you are able to edge join an item that has only one flat surface (the one you'll put into the fence) Two smooth, straight, and adjacent surfaces offers more possibilities for feeding the stock through the jointer. Therefore, I highly recommend flattening opposite sides of the thickness planeer. There is no requirement in this stage to get the boards down until the thickness that you want to achieve.

Chapter 15: Machined Joints

Scarf joints

The use of scarf joints has been used to construct wooden boats for many years. There are a variety of variations to the type of joint; some variants comprise tabbed, feathered as well as hooked scarfs. In addition, there are a variety of

solutions for them, ranging including bringing planks together for the construction of longest length staves made from small pieces.

Thanks to the advancements in engineering for structural construction, which resulted in lighter vessels, and also significant advances in glues, the properties and capabilities when they are compared to or paired with the solid wood must be understood.

The scarves' description is based on the amount of slopes that are about the piece's hardness that are paired to form a relationship. This is referred to as a simple ratio.

Below are some instances of how to apply a scarf joint

Bevel-cut scarves

If you break the edges of angles the angle is exposed to an additional long grain, which can be used to strengthen bonds. The more blunt the angle, the greater and stronger the surface for gluing. For example, a 45deg bevel increases the value of the gluing surface by forty percent. It also helps to hide the joint line when placed on the surface that is neatly cut. For a perfect alignment with the angles, cut an end of the blade on one side of the saw blade, and the end that is mating to the opposite side. If your blade's bevel angle alters from 45deg to 45deg, the parts will remain being matched.

Miter-cut scarves

Make this joint to create the largest and wider glue surface. Begin by making the 4:1 angle guide which is more than double the size of the two work pieces. Similar cleats to both sides of the triangle assist in positioning across the surface of the two pieces. The angles on the workpieces should be recorded and then bandsaw them until they are within 1/32" of the lines of scrap sides.

It is a huge smooth, machine-cut joint to do small batch jobs such as the edges of wooden frames. The slip joint is a similar fundamental geometry in its surface or face as a conventional Bridle Joint, however it's made with a unique way. The slim, large proportions are able to offer a huge area of gluing.

A slip joint can be made by the use of the bandsaw along with some preparation, the possibility to create a variety of identical suitable slip joints becomes possible for all. When a joint is perfectly fitted then everything else becomes simple. One of the main uses for an slip joint is frames with corners that are low profile. Frames need sturdy wood that won't twist or bow during any change in the humidity level. It is possible to prepare the wood using basic hand tools or equipment, If you're using an electronic planer you should round it off using a hand plane following. Use the grain of the wood to eliminate any striations on the surface.

Prepare yourself to make an initial thought The secret to creating fitting slip joints that are well-fitted lies within the shims' toughness. After the shims have been well-maintained, keep them in the same condition and each joint you use afterwards will perfectly.

Biscuits and biscuits

This joint is a strengthened butt joint, which has an oval-shaped shape. A biscuit is composed from well-compacted and dried wood, similar to the beech used for the two pieces of timber that are used to match mortises and the Tenons. Most people make use of a biscuit jointer to construct matching mortises instances where accuracy isn't essential. The purpose of this joint is to allow for flexibility when glueing.

Scribed joint

The joint that is ascribed to use where two moldings meet at an inner corner. In lieu of being mitered the piece's end is shaped to match the shape of the opposite piece. The scribed joint can also be called coping joints and coping saws were designed specifically for this use. The use of the scribed joint can be seen when the installation of skirting boards. For instance, it's best practice to utilize the scribed joint on all internal corrosion angle and an additional kind of joint, called the miter joint, which is for external angles. The reason for this is that wood can shrink as it gets wider, which could make the miter joints open to the inside. This isn't a great effect.

Special joint

Chinese chair Joint

Chinese furniture is in use for quite a while. Furniture made of lacquer was present in Han dynasty's tombs in the beginning of around 206 B.C. and during the Southern and Northern Dynasties from (420-589) and under the influence of Buddhists and the Buddhists, the Chinese began to adopt the custom of sitting down on platform-like platforms and seated in a seated position with their feet pointing upwards on chairs or a stool.

It is a luxurious mortise and Tenon technique as well as its durability as well as seamlessness and strength creation of joints made from wood. It is, however, a fashionable and sophisticated method of construction, it's longevity is reasons the majority woodworkers continue to employ it up to today. This isn't new, as Chinese Architects have put mortise and tenon joinery in the construction of houses and for other work for many years. This is the reason why this design was used until the present mostly due to its dependability and the simplicity of building. In the absence of material for fixing, the quality of the construction is maintained throughout the life of.

Indeed, although it is the case that different Chinese Dynasties have been implemented and have been distributed in the field of design for buildings, Chinese joinery is still unchanging. It's been tested as a recipe and has become a household label of cabinet makers. Therefore, when furniture from China arrives at your door the strength and durability is evident. Mortise and tenon techniques are very popular in China due to its rarity and straightforward type of joinery.

cornice joint

Coving, cornice, and architrave are words which are frequently used in improperly or in a way that makes them appear to be the same thing.

A cornice can be described as a moulding used to conceal the joints formed between ceilings and the wall. This guarantees that it won't need to be finished. It also ensures that any kind of crack or asymmetry is hidden.

The cornice may be simple or quite

fashioned. The plain cornice may be used occasionally

known as 'coving.'

Coving and cornice are made of plaster and paper-covered plasters, polyurethane as well as a variety of others.

An architrave is one type of moulding that is placed on top of a window or door or other type of opening. In the case of an architrave, it extends over the top of the side moldings towards the opening. The term "architrave" is used to refer to the horizontal and upright moldings which form the structure of the door, window or any other opening in the industry of building. The term architrave can be derived from wood.

Green woodworking joint

Another type of woodcrafting is Green woodworking, or more precisely, carpentry. This is about turning green or unseasoned timber into different forms, or furniture. Unseasoned wood is the type that's just been cut down or preserved through maintaining the wood in a trough that is filled with water to ensure its increasing amount of water. The green wood is soft compared to seasoned wood which makes it much simpler to form using hand equipment. When the wood that is not seasoned has lost its moisture content shrinkage takes place as well, and green woodworkers is able to use this shrinkage in order to ensure that joints are tight for their businesses. To enhance the effects of shrinkage the one side of a joint might be dried over in a kiln, while the another component remains with a green. The parts tighten each other as they exchange moisture with their immediate surrounding. The expansion of the Tenon in the expanding "green" mortise creates a extremely strong, secure permanently bonded joint, even although adhesives aren't readily offered. A different traditional green woodworking task is bodging. In the past, components of chairs were made straight from woods, before being transported to workshops in which the chairs were joined with the help of cabinetmakers. Woodworking in the green has enjoyed an upswing due to the media's influence as well as the advent of the hand-tool woodworking revolution.

Chapter 16: What Is Woodworking?

It's the creation of objects out of wood with the power or hand tools. The process of woodworking is much more complicated than what it appears at first and encompasses everything from simple green woodworking through to intricate and precise cabinet making. Woodworking is the term used to refer to the process by most people. However, within the industry it is more a reference to the building of woodwork for institutional use in residential construction that is typically done on-site. Woodworkers who create doors and windows as well as similar things are known as bench joiners. They typically work in the conference room. An experienced woodworker is able to maximize the use different materials, ranging including natural wood to plywood and standard. The key isn't just to be proficient using tools, but also planning and design.

Wood is a pliable wood that, with the least number of tools, it could be among the first materials used for shelters and other equipment. There's a broad range varieties of wood types that are available in various grades, and, for the majority of traditional research, it must be dried in order so that it is not moved after the wood has been used. There are various woodworkers that specialize like chairs, barrel makers, woodcarvers, shipwrights and wheelwrights and makers of instruments. Art comes with its own special equipment, such as chairmakers have travisers for creating hollowed chair seats in order so that they are more comfortable and wooden carvers can use various gouges to cut different designs. Techniques of woodworking allow us to design and build things that range from houses to furniture, boats and doors, as well as windows, animals' housing, workbenches, tools and frame frames for pictures, toys containers, and much more.

Woodworking comes with a wide assortment too. A part of the job can be joined with only nails, or with exquisitely-crafted joints. Wooden structures found that are used in homes are typically joined by screws and nails, however the chair or older home may have mortice or Tenon joints. Professionally trained woodworkers make use of a variety of various joints in various scenarios to withstand the different pressures that is applied to their piece. Some examples of joints are mitre, bridle, fingers box, housing dovetail, butt and groove, mortice and lapping, halving, or tenon joints. Certain ligaments can be easily repaired using hand tools. However, other require power tools, like domino or biscuit joints. These are made for speed and efficiency, but can be very durable.

What should I do?

It doesn't need cost a lot. Wood is readily available that is often for free when you get a good forester or landowner, or even if you reuse old pieces. We recommend you beware of MDF because it has toxic additives like formaldehyde which means there's dangers to your health when cutting it. Sometimes, making use of other materials made by humans, such as plywood is logical - it's far more effective for creating boxes like cabinets, kitchens, and even cabinets. Solid wood for that circumstance is an unnecessary waste.

Join a woodworking workshop to develop skills and assurance that you are aware of how to tackle an assignment. There is no need for a lot of equipment - simply start building up your skills as time passes. It's not just an entire workshop.

What exactly is a woodworker?

A woodworker makes a variety of products, including cabinetry (cabinet makers) as well as furniture (furniture finishing) constructed from wood as well as synthetic wood. The term "woodworker" can also refer to carpenters.

There were two myths about woodworkers.

These assumptions, thankfully, do not hold anymore. Today, there is more choice of woodworking tools than there ever was thanks to the online community as well as the accessibility of equipment and supplies.

Over the past ten years, we have seen an enormous increase in quantity of woodworkers taking up as a pastime, most foremost, females. There wasn't a long time back that woodworking by women was considered to be a rare thing. Woodworkers of women are now commonplace. You can't find anything that a person cannot do make by woodworking.

Another major shift in demographics was seen among the millennials males in their in their 20s or 30s. There are people I know working within Silicon Valley all the time or are doing an office job of some sort or job, but feel the urge to use their hands.

Despite the numerous metals, plastics as well as other sources wood-based products continue to be a major element of our life. Most of the items mentioned can be mass-produced, like kitchen cabinets, chairs and even musical equipment. Some items are made to order using special equipment at small stores.

What does a woodworker do?

The most common woodworkers do is:

Explore the full schematics and blueprints.

Set up and prepare equipment.

Use devices to lift wood parts using a hand, or by using hoists.

Utilize cutting and wood-making equipment.

Be aware of unusual sound or notice excessive vibrating.

Make sure the products meet specifications, and then make adjustments if required.

Make use of hand tools for cutting pieces or to mount items.

Clean and replace the rusty blades of your saw.

The term " woodworker "can conjure images of a skilled craftsman building elaborate furniture with hand tools, today's woodworking industry is highly complex and involves the use of highly-skilled equipment and workers. The workers use automated equipment including computers with numeric control (CNC) tools that do the bulk of their work. However, skilled artisans generally use many equipment for power work. A lot of research is carried out in an production line, however there is still research that is specific and is not suited to being made on the assembly line.

Woodworkers can be found in any part of the secondary wood products industry From the sawmill up to the final products, and their responsibilities vary. They are the ones who set up, manage and oversee all kinds of equipment for woodworking including drilling presses and lathes shapers, routers and sanders as well as planers and wood-nailing equipment. Operators setup the machinery, create and cut wooden pieces and check the dimensions with a template, a calliper, or rule.

When wood components are created then woodworkers use fasteners and adhesives, and join the parts to form a complete assembled. Then, they sand, stain and, if needed finish the product with a sealer for example, a lacquer or varnish.

Have you been trained to become a woodworker?

Woodworkers are distinguished by their characteristics. They're typically artists, meaning that they're intuitive, creative as well as articulate, sensitive and evocative.

They're free of structure, innovative as well as non-conformist and imaginative. A few of them tend to be observer-like, meaning they're contemplative, analytical and keen.

Does this appear like you? Check out our job match check to see whether woodworker can be one of the top career opportunities.

What's the working environment like for woodworkers?

The job assignments differ according to various work assignments. In most cases, employees have to transport heavy, bulky items which can cause lots of dust and noise. The employees also use earplugs, boots and glasses to protect their eyes. Some work all day outside of the normal business hours.

What's The Difference Between A "Maker" And A "Woodworker"?

Maker is a fairly brand new concept that's been popping over the last decade or more.

The term encompasses all those who are interested with various arts and arts and crafts. It could be work in wood, metalworking, concreting, epoxying programming and telecommunications, 3D printing weaving, baking spin, making jewellery and sculpting, ceramics robots, as well as using Legos. In essence, we're all makers.

Woodworkers are builders who's main interest is developing and enhancing the craft making products from wood. There are times when we incorporate equipment in our designs, however our focus is always on wood. It's a cost-effective, long-lasting product that is easy to build using.

What's the Difference Between Cabinet Making as well as Furniture Making?

In the end, there's no clear line that connects the two terms because, I believe that cabinet builders build things which are built in places, for instance kitchen cabinets, and focus more on the materials that are obvious.

Furniture is able to be put wherever the user would like, later, additional sections of the completed product may be placed on the market.

Cabinets may use plywood more than other furniture, and they is constructed with screws as well as other fasteners. Furniture usually utilizes solid lumber, and usually has higher quality joints and glue. Furniture manufacturing may need more accuracy.

There is plenty of overlapping here. I've made a lot of furniture from screws and plywood, and I've seen incredible cabinets that compete with the best furniture.

SECRETS FOR OUTDOOR WOODWORKING

If you're looking to construct a patio or swing set, gazebo or another outdoor wood construction this time of year it is possible that you are going to be a victim of loss without being aware of that. I can remember having to endure many heartbreaks trying to figure out how to prevent loss in the most difficult method. It's not a good idea to finish with finishes that aren't durable and joints that split and surfaces stained by corrosion are regular and painful fates encountered in the majority of outdoor woodworking ventures. They are popular indeed and not unavoidable, in any case, If you adhere to my tested field techniques for design and construction.

Be dry and dark The sun and the moisture are both enemies of the wood and dealing effectively with them starts at the beginning of the season. That's why cedar is an ideal option for projects outdoors. It's resistant to rot and lasts for a long time However, cedar comes with its own disadvantages. It's particularly soft which has implications for how you design your.

Round: Cedar dents quickly, which is why it's logical for rounding corners using the help of a router. Straight edges do not carry an edge as those that are curved or rounded which is why a worn-out corner's surface can lead to degrading to adjoining zones.

Wood screws with wide diameters: Large diameter screws for wood - I prefer #10 - are better suited to cedar since the wood is so beautiful. Even these screws must be secured with weatherproof glue and not only to strength.

Find the best glue Regular wood glues, including those that have been classified as water-resistant get mushy when wet or dry. The reason glue makers offer types II and III wooden glues. They're third-party labels that are issued through the American National Standards Institute (ANSI) in order to guarantee that glue joints are strong, even through weeks of dry conditions. The only adhesive used was for these labels specifically for outdoor activities. Applying cement to the hammered, fixed and fitted joints of your furniture outside can make your final product more durable. But glue makes the furniture last longer due to its ability to trap the moisture.

Use glue to keep insects away: Every aspect can affect how glue can be applied for outdoor activities. Make sure you cover the joint, not just a couple of dab in and out. Also, when planning outdoor furniture, make the smallest gaps between the pieces as you are able to. Certain regions in Canada the spaces are the perfect environment for insect creatures that leave mounds that are small and coarse black droppings that hold water and promote rapid decay due to the nutrients that they offer. But, who would want to lay on a lawnchair full of manure?

The first choice of fasteners: Fastener choice is a different issue. Although most screws and nails have a type of golden, silver, or green coating, which suggests the protection against corrosion, very few fasteners can effectively stop staining and corrosion over the long term. That's why I'm an avid lover of steel-based screws as well as nails. They were once impossible to find and aren't anymore. Screws, finishing nails as well as frame nails are found in corrosion-resistant stainless. Outdoor furniture joints that require larger bolts, you can use heat dipped steel carriage bolts galvanized. These bolts have a mottled aged grey color that performs similarly to stainless steel. However, be sure to take off shiny silver electroplated screws washers, and nuts. These are more sought-after over galvanized with a heat dip as well as costing less, however they do corrode, and stain wood with shocking levels. Be aware of the type of fastener used. It is crucial when you're working with pressure treated lumber. The additives for preservation create a substance that is 10 times more corrosive natural wood.

The Secrets You Need To Know When Using Wood In Wet Spaces

What if you said that moisture and wood aren't compatible?

It's not logical, in fact, to practice of using a material such as wood, which is prone to expansion and humidity in an area that is constantly being soaked, such as the kitchen, bathroom or the outside of a structure. But with an in-depth review and a selection of appropriate plants it is suitable for nearly any place that is dry or wet. We examine five areas where the usage of wood might seem debatable initially. We'll examine the reasons why wood is suitable for this area or location.

Siding and wood shingles

It's rare to see wooden sidings on the exterior of a house before. when you look at the practice, it could be a bit odd. What is the reason to put wood siding on the exterior of a house, but do not cover it in paint? What can it do to prevent it from rotting and dying when exposed to the elements of rain and snow? There is a fact that there are a few species of wood appropriate for siding on exteriors, however, the type of wood species that we describe as cedar is an but rare exception.

The term "cedar" is a reference to a mixture of more than 12 varieties of trees which belong to different families. they wished to share the same traits of resistance to decay and rot because of "resins" or "extractives" within the wood. These are natural chemicals created by the trees. This ensures there is no requirement to dye, paint or even pre-treat the wood, which keeps the wood from rotting and decay even though the wood may change colour and age and eventually turn a greyish shade contrast to the reddish and brown hues that shingles begin in their lifespan. It's not a guarantee that non-painted wood siding will never get rusty, but with the proper design and decoration by spacing the shingles to allow water to flow from the shingle instead of taking up water beneath it the siding can last for many years.

Wood roofing

Installing shingles or siding made of wood for roofing can appear odder than wood siding. However, there are certain rules to follow in this regard: You want to ensure that you're selecting a wood type which is resistant to moisture and the wood has been placed or treated in the appropriate way.

Roofs made of wood are not as popular than siding made of wood, however when the period of colonial America that was when they were the most popular type of roofing materials. Today, they 're still used, particularly in projects that want to create a traditional-meets-modern look or in places where cedar is simple to access and fairly inexpensive. The idea of wood roofing is as being more environmentally conscious over other materials. This is due to the fact that it is a renewable resource, and cedar roof shingles come with the potential to last for over 60 years (when they are properly maintained and cared for). In the beginning, if your wood roof starts showing the signs of moss or mildew it is possible to purchase outside spray applications that could be used to correct the issue.

Wooden kitchen countertops

When compared to other material like concrete, wood countertops might appear unsuitable or dangerous, especially if they are used within the sink area in which water keeps spilling over the edges, and the pans, pots and utensils begin to accumulate. But countertops constructed from wood such as butcher blocks (a wood-based sheet that has been laminated) are widely used over the years. Wood countertops, regardless of whether they're made from solid wood, such as broad slabs of walnut or traditional butcher block made of maple, will give a dry and natural appearance in kitchens as well as reduce the noise of pans and pots being dropped upon the counter.

However, this doesn't mean any kind of wood makes excellent countertops or that there's minimal or any maintenance required. The softer varieties of wood such as oak do not make the best countertops due to how easily they break and scratch. It is, however, possible to apply the sandpaper method to finish wood that has damaged, the process of refinishing the entire countertop damaged or scratched can be difficult, and even impossible by using tougher types of wood like beech, birch, or maple are chosen. Also, wooden countertops could be cleaned once a month, if the surface remains not finished, or it can be refinished each five years when it comes already finished at the manufacturer. It will protect the wood from stains that are a result of water use, however it will need regular maintenance.

Bathrooms with wood surfaces

Due to the constant humidity of bathrooms, wood is not the first choice for many in selecting an appropriate finish for the bathroom especially since ceramic tiles or other non-porous surfaces can be found in an array of colors and costs. But, thanks to the fresh and natural appearance and warm to the touch unlike the harshness of tiles wooden floors are becoming an increasingly popular choice for bathrooms?

Wood is often used for an interior wall, floor or ceiling finishing in bathrooms -- particularly one that has a tub or shower, it is important to ensure there's a fan to provide adequate ventilation. This will prevent the wood from bending and also reduce the possibility of mildew or mould growing. A second tip is to ensure that the wood is covered with any kind of sealant, perhaps boiling linseed oil or the urethane sealant, in order to protect it from further damage. Also, be sure to have all of the ends covered although they may not necessarily be apparent. Some experts suggest adding the tar sheet (usually found under roofing shingles) prior to constructing the timber to add an additional protection and insulation.

Wooden bathtubs

Then, we come to the greatest mystery of the bunch: a bathtub made of wood. The tub constructed of wood seems as if it's going to be constantly leaking or expand enough that it is no longer a shape. Yet, a variety of communities across all over the world have been building wooden tubs for generations In particular, the Japanese are known to have utilized fragrant woods such as cedar and hinoki to make bathtubs that soak, known as ofuro in addition, teak and different woods are used to make tubs across Scandinavian nations.

The most important thing to consider when making the bathtub made of wood as with the other types of use for woodit is to ensure that the appropriate varieties of wood are chosen right from the start and also that the wood is regularly kept in good condition. For instance, teak was primarily used for the decks of ships. It also works effectively as a tub material due to its resistance to the ravages of rot. There are some experts who advocate for using several coats of sealant for bathtubs made of wood to provide continuous assurance from the wet-dry cycles they traverse, and will create a rougher than it was. This allows hair or skin cells to be trapped inside the wood.

Chapter 18: Tools And Techniques Of Outdoor Wood Project

The ideas included in the book seem to be relatively small. Therefore, they can all be built with inexpensive timber, simple bolts and screws, circular saws or an handsaw. Even a tiny investment or a couple of hours of work will yield finished products that are stunning and will look great for quite a while.

In the beginning, less expensive varieties of wood may be brimming with moisture this means that they will weaken and cause ugly gaps between joints, as well as cracks and warping. This chapter will help you choose boards that keep their attractive appearance and strength. Also, we'll discuss fastening tools which is more secure and appear better than normal screws and nails.

If you own a tool set that is handyman-like such as, for instance circular saws and a hand mitre boxes, you could build most of these items. To make your projects flow more efficiently and produce more appealing result, you might want to invest a couple of dollars to upgrade your tools a bit, such as a jig with a pocket screw, an accessory that has a straight-hole to drill or a higher-quality hand-mitre box. You can also go for a more advanced method that will can make you feel like a professional, such as the power mitre saw, or table saw.

Whatever tools that you choose to use, you'll likely get superior results by learning and applying tried-and-tested building techniques. The majority of these strategies are easy to master which can extend the construction process by a few minutes. However, it could be the difference between a clearly inexperienced item and one that looks as though it was constructed by the woodshop.

Choosing Wood

In light of the rising usage of synthetic and vinyl building materials wood's inherent appeal wood is appealing to the majority of us.

It's impossible to match the distinctive grain patterns you'll find on a might board made from real wood. Wood surfaces, even if they may be a bit scratched or distorted -- possess distinct charm and warmth, and can make your outdoor area seem than just a relaxing escape away from your daily routine.

However, even though we do not be looking for perfection but we need forums that can keep their opening statements without obvious wrinkles. A lot of trellises and plants begin to appear untidy after a short time.

Choosing the best lumber, and maybe applying a short coat of finishing each year is a good way to prevent that from happening.

Wood Species

The idea of making an outdoor design made of raw oak fir, or hem-fi-r is possible, however wet rot is almost certain to happen unless you use large quantity of preservative, mortar as well as polish or paint and cover the wood by holy enthusiasm. These plants possess a natural tolerance to rot However, they can be used if they are in a sealed.

Redwood and Cedar

Western red cedar is available at fair prices across the majority of regions of the globe. (Other varieties, like oriental white, incense as well as northern white, are not available locally.) It's fairly softit is often damaged it by pressing hard using your thumb -- but it's strong enough that it can be a deck material. The wood is susceptible to cracking, however this is generally not the case.

A major issue to consider when you choose boards with care and make pilot holes prior to installing fasteners close to the board's endpoints. The dark heartwood of the board is susceptible to rotting, however the sapwood that is lighter in colour isn't as permeable. If it is necessary, pick the darker boards. However, cedar must be coated with stain and then secured to prevent it from decay.

There is a wide range of cedar grades that could be possible. Search for terms such as " heart " and " tight knot.

The most expensive cedar " clear heart "has no knots and can be extremely costly. Boards that have the label " S4S "are flawless on all four sides however, other boards could appear rough on only the one side.

Boards that have the label " 5-1/2 decking "are 1 inch. Thick and 51/2 inches. Wide. This is a good and affordable option for many initiatives. These boards have edges with rounded edges. They will create clearly visible lines in the event that two boards are pressed to each other.

Redwood is available all over the globe. If the lumberyard you are using stock it, they'll likely purchase it. It's extremely durable and susceptible to splitting. It is also extremely durable, which makes it more durable than cedar However, it's typically higher priced. Similar to cedar, heartwood with the dark color can stand up to further rot than light sapwood.

There are a variety of varieties of redwood, however most retailers only stock a few in the best case. The ones that include the words " typical "include at the very least a portion of sapwood. Other " heart " or " all heart " types are darker and more durable. A top grade, Clear All Soul, could be too expensive;

If you want a lovely knotty appearance and a high rot resistance maybe go with Construction Heart or Merchantable Heart.

www.ingramcontent.com/pod-product-compliance
Lightning Source LLC
Chambersburg PA
CBHW071448080526
44587CB00014B/2034